CITYSPOTS

BELFAST

WHAT'S IN YOUR GUIDEBOOK?

Independent authors Impartial up-to-date information from our travel experts who meticulously source local knowledge.

Experience Thomas Cook's 165 years in the travel industry and guidebook publishing enriches every word with expertise you can trust.

Travel know-how Thomas Cook has thousands of staff working around the globe, all living and breathing travel.

Editors Travel-publishing professionals, pulling everything together to craft a perfect blend of words, pictures, maps and design.

You, the traveller We deliver a practical, no-nonsense approach to information, geared to how you really use it.

ABOUT THE AUTHOR

Based in County Down, Northern Ireland, Louise McGrath (aka Pole-Baker) is a freelance writer/editor and the author of Thomas Cook's *CitySpots Belfast* and *Lisbon* guides. Louise writes regularly for *www.whatsonwhen.com*, working on web content for major airlines and hotel chains. She has lived in Colombia, Spain and Florida, and in her spare time likes to walk in the Mourne Mountains, practise yoga and listen to live music.

CITYSPOTS
BELFAST
Louise McGrath

Thomas Cook

Written by Louise McGrath

Published by Thomas Cook Publishing
A division of Thomas Cook Tour Operations Limited
Company registration No: 1450464 England
The Thomas Cook Business Park, 9 Coningsby Road
Peterborough PE3 8SB, United Kingdom
Email: books@thomascook.com, Tel: +44 (0)1733 416477
www.thomascookpublishing.com

Produced by The Content Works Ltd
Aston Court, Kingsmead Business Park, Frederick Place
High Wycombe, Bucks HP11 1LA
www.thecontentworks.com

Series design based on an original concept by Studio 183 Limited

ISBN: 978-1-84848-040-7

First edition © 2006 Thomas Cook Publishing
This second edition © 2009 Thomas Cook Publishing
Text © Thomas Cook Publishing
Maps © Thomas Cook Publishing/PCGraphics (UK) Limited
Northern Ireland maps: reproduced by permission of the Ordnance Survey of
Northern Ireland on behalf of the Controller of Her Majesty's Stationery Office
© Crown copyright 2008 (Permit No. 80151)
Transport map © Communicarta Limited

Series Editor: Lucy Armstrong
Production/DTP: Steven Collins

Printed and bound in Spain by GraphyCems

Cover photography (The Speaker at Custom House) © Tom Steventon/Alamy

CONTENTS

SYMBOLS KEY

The following symbols are used throughout this book:

ⓐ address ☏ telephone ⓕ fax ⓦ website address ⓔ email
🕒 opening times ⓝ public transport connections ❶ important

The following symbols are used on the maps:

ℹ information office		▪ points of interest	
✈ airport		◯ city	
✚ hospital		◯ large town	
Ⓤ police station		○ small town	
🚍 bus station		═ motorway	
🚆 railway station		— main road	
✝ cathedral		— minor road	
❶ numbers denote featured cafés & restaurants		— railway	

Hotels and restaurants are graded by approximate price as follows:
£ budget price **££** mid-range price **£££** expensive

▶ *The Big Fish sculpture at Donegall Quay*

Introduction

Belfast is buzzing. Not since the height of the Industrial Revolution, when it was given its city status by Queen Victoria, has it seen such a period of optimism. Today Belfast is shaking off its violent image and projecting itself as a vibrant city with plenty to offer the visitor, from art, history and green spaces to fine dining, café culture and trendy bars. Even the notorious Falls and Shankill Roads are seeing a piece of the new action, with sightseeing buses and 'ex-prisoner' tours taking visitors to the political murals of West Belfast.

Belfast is the largest city in Northern Ireland, but with a relatively small population, the urban area can be easily explored on foot. It's also not difficult to get out of the city for a day or two if you want to head north along the stunning Antrim Coast to Giant's Causeway or south to County Down and the Mourne Mountains.

From the landmark City Hall in Donegall Square you can shop your way along Royal Avenue, over to the Cathedral Quarter and along High Street to Custom House Square. You can enjoy riverside walks along the Lagan, picnics in the Botanic Gardens and mini hikes to McArt's Fort in Cave Hill Country Park. There's interactive fun at the Odyssey complex, classical concerts at the Waterfront Hall and live bands at the Limelight. Tuck into an Ulster fry for breakfast, snack on seafood chowder and wheaten bread for lunch and sample some modern Irish cuisine for dinner, then bar hop down the Golden Mile to Botanic Avenue for some of that notorious Irish *craic*.

These days there's little to keep you away from Belfast. The new-found optimism has meant regeneration and an increase in the number of budget airlines flying to the two nearby airports. When you arrive you'll find the people warm and welcoming to visitors, keeping their identity and history firmly in sight, while looking forward with a contagious sense of enthusiasm.

◗ *Waterfront Hall from the River Lagan*

When to go

Although sunstroke won't be a major worry, summer days can be lovely, and the warmth of the welcome from the local people will soothe even the wettest winter chill. Belfast's manifold charms are not weather-dependent. Swing by any time: you'll love it.

SEASONS & CLIMATE

Located in Belfast Lough, which leads out to the Irish Sea, Belfast has a temperate maritime climate, with four distinct seasons. The general vibe tends towards the moist, with an annual rainfall of 85 cm (33½ in). Summer temperatures average around 17.5°C (63½°F); winter temperatures around 6°C (43°F).

● *Crowds flock to open-air concerts at City Hall*

ANNUAL EVENTS

January
Out to Lunch Brought to you by the organisers of May's Cathedral Quarter Arts Festival (see below), this is a city-wide, month-long arts festival that turns up many a gem. Ⓦ www.cqaf.com/outtolunch

March
St Patrick's Day (17 Mar) It wasn't until 1998 that Belfast started having its own city-centre celebrations for Ireland's patron saint, including concerts by renowned musicians such as Shane McGowan on stage outside the City Hall. In 2006, the carnival moved to Custom House Square.

May
Cathedral Quarter Arts Festival Fringe theatre and performing arts groups, as well as music, comedy, film, circus acts and visual arts events take over the city's pubs and arts venues for the month. Ⓦ www.cqaf.com

The Balmoral Show (Usually mid-month) Ireland's largest agricultural show, featuring a children's farm, dog agility competitions, falconry displays, livestock, Pony Club games, sheep shearing, show jumping and gun dog displays.
ⓐ Balmoral Showgrounds Ⓦ www.balmoralshow.co.uk

June
Beat Summer Carnival (Late June) A cross-community event in Custom House Square, with a carnival parade, floats, bands, dancers and cultural groups from diverse sections of the community.
Ⓣ 028 9046 0865 Ⓦ www.belfastcarnival.com

July

Orangefest On 12 July, the Orange Order celebrates the victory of William of Orange over James I in 1690 with 'demonstrations'. The Belfast demonstrations are the largest in Northern Ireland and see Orange Order flute bands parading through the city centre and south to Edenderry Field for speeches. To promote things from a generally cuddlier angle and appeal to a wider audience, the event has been rebranded as 'Orangefest'. Ⓦ www.belfastorange.com

Belfast International Rose Trials and Rose Week at Sir Thomas and Lady Dixon Park (Late July) This attracts 50,000 visitors for the serious rose competition as well as fun activities for children, from face painting to treasure hunts. Ⓦ www.belfastcity.gov.uk/rosegardentour

August

Belfast Pride Mainly – but not exclusively – gay-themed jamboree that sees a week of arts and culture events culminating in a colourful parade through the city centre. Ⓦ www.belfastpride.com

West Belfast Festival (Féile an Phobail) The largest community-led festival in Europe, with internationally renowned musicians, exhibitions, debates, drama events, an international food fair and a parade. Ⓦ www.feilebelfast.com

September

Coors Light Open House Festival (Late Sept) The Cathedral Quarter celebrates the Open House Festival: traditional arts with a focus on music events from Irish traditional to bluegrass, Cajun and country. Ⓦ www.openhousefestival.com

October

Belfast Festival at Queen's Ireland's largest arts festival comes to Queen's each year, with an impressive programme of events featuring renowned and up-and-coming performers and artists, cutting edge performances and special projects in theatre, dance, music, visual art, film and spoken word throughout the city.
Ⓦ www.belfastfestival.com

November

Belfast Book Fair Book lovers flock here for the country's biggest and longest-running book fair, with dozens of dealers doing a good trade in secondhand, rare and antiquarian publications.
ⓘ 028 9038 1111 Ⓦ www.wellingtonparkhotel.com
CineMagic World Screen Festival for Young People Month-long, city-wide screen fest for kids. Ⓦ www.cinemagic.org.uk

PUBLIC HOLIDAYS
New Year's Day 1 Jan
St Patrick's Day 17 Mar
Good Friday 10 Apr 2009; 2 Apr 2010; 22 Apr 2011
Easter Monday 13 Apr 2009; 5 Apr 2010; 25 Apr 2011
May Bank Holiday first Mon in May
Spring Bank Holiday last Mon in May
Battle of the Boyne 12 July
August Bank Holiday last Mon in Aug
Christmas Day 25 Dec
Boxing Day 26 Dec

Rebirth of Belfast

The new optimism felt in Belfast since the Good Friday Agreement and devolution in 2007 has resonated throughout the city, attracting investment into run-down areas. The first 'new builds' included the BT Tower, Hilton Hotel and apartments on Laganside, plus the landmark Odyssey Complex and Science Park which have made inroads into the Titanic Quarter. In 2008, the multi-million pound Victoria Square shopping centre opened in the heart of Belfast. The centre is an architectural masterpiece that blends Belfast's Victorian architecture with 21st-century style, and adds to the city's attractiveness as a city-break destination.

The redevelopment of the former Gasworks 'brown site' into a landscaped showpiece with offices, the Radisson Hotel, housing and cafés has been hailed as a major success. Custom House Square has also had a makeover, giving it new life and opening it up to live events and festivals. The Grand Opera House has been extended and improved, and the former Ulster Bank in the Cathedral Quarter has been transformed into the elegant Merchant Hotel.

The regeneration and construction that has already taken place is just the beginning. Over the next two decades the Titanic Quarter is to be transformed into a new maritime quarter, adding cafés and bars, retail space, apartments, hotel and office buildings, as well as a new quay at Abercorn Basin, community facilities, and public art and event spaces.

Laganside is to see further regeneration, turning it into a vibrant nightlife and entertainment area, plus the construction of Obel Tower at Donegall Quay, set to be Northern Ireland's tallest building.

The Ulster Museum rejuvenation project has brought a new entrance and arrival space, improved history and natural science galleries and a new rooftop gallery, plus a new café and restaurant. The Old Museum Arts Centre awaits its move to a new, purpose-built site in the Cathedral Quarter in 2011. City Hall is also receiving essential attention to maintain its prized Victorian interiors.

The city centre was a virtual no-go area at night before the Good Friday Agreement. While the political future is still being defined, construction and regeneration of the city has made its residents feel a sense of renewal, and this optimism has continued since devolution in 2007. Tourists generally feel happier to visit Belfast and it has become one of the hottest city-break destinations in the United Kingdom.

● *Regeneration continues to transform the city centre*

History

Belfast's name derives from the Gaelic *Béal Feirste*, meaning 'sandy ford at the mouth of the River Farset'. The location of the Farset, now contained within a pipe under High Street, is the oldest part of the city: John de Courcy built a castle here in the 12th century; in 1611 Baron Arthur Chichester built another on the same site, which was destroyed in a fire in 1708.

Chichester encouraged the plantation of Ulster by English and Scottish Protestant Planters, but during the Irish Uprising of 1641, thousands of these Planters were massacred, and many fled back to England. James II became King of Ireland in 1685 but the arrival of William of Orange saw support by Ulster, where there was a Protestant majority. James was defeated in 1690 and penal laws were brought in, curbing the rights of Catholics.

By the early 18th century, Belfast was a large settlement, the arrival of French Huguenots stimulating the growth of the linen industry. One of their descendents, the philanthropist and radical Henry Joy McCracken, formed the United Irishmen with Theobold Wolfe Tone. Their aim was to end oppressive English rule, but following their 1798 rebellion at the Battle of Antrim, McCracken was captured and hanged.

During the 19th century the Industrial Revolution led to growth in shipbuilding, ropeworks, tobacco factories and linen mills, and Belfast receiving city status by royal decree. With new employment opportunities and the devastating effects of the Potato Famine in rural areas, people flooded into the city, settling in areas that were already predominantly either Catholic or Protestant. Unrest continued into the new century, and following the Irish War of

Independence, most of Ulster saw partition from the South and the creation of Northern Ireland with Belfast as its capital.

The city continued to grow, becoming the world's most important shipbuilding location. However, Belfast was severely bombed during World War II, and the post-war period saw jobs drying up as air travel began to supersede sea travel.

Old religious prejudices led to Civil Rights marches by Catholics and riots by Loyalist gangs, culminating in the British Army's deployment to keep the peace in 1969. Direct Rule by the British Government replaced the Northern Ireland government and the period known as The Troubles continued for almost 30 years, with violence by the IRA, loyalist UVF and other paramilitary groups. After peace talks with republican party Sinn Féin, and an IRA ceasefire, the Good Friday Agreement was put into place in 1998, leading to the creation of the Northern Ireland Assembly. This was suspended by the British Government in 2002, but after years of negotiations devolution of power was achieved in 2007. Under the power-sharing agreement DUP's Ian Paisley became First Minister and Sinn Féin's Martin McGuinness his Deputy. Paisley retired in 2008.

⬤ *The imposing façade of Stormont Castle*

Lifestyle

In the past decade the city centre has undergone a physical transformation and the lifestyle of many of Belfast's residents has also improved. The city centre is now open and vibrant with a booming café culture, new bars, restaurants, shops and cultural venues. Even the Falls and Shankill roads have become attractions as tourists take guided tours to see the political murals, something that would have seemed unlikely as little as a decade ago. Despite this, the political future remains uncertain and with The Troubles still in the memories of most of the population, old rivalries and fears persist.

Many children still go to Catholic or Protestant schools and therefore identity is defined by community, with sports, music, language and even the football team supported dictated by education and religion. Growing numbers of integrated schools and cross-community projects are working tirelessly to promote mutual understanding and transcend these rivalries.

In the Cathedral Quarter, city centre and South Belfast you really have a feel of this transformation, an excitement about the changes and the benefits of a newly affluent society. Students from both communities meet at college and begin to understand each other, while equal opportunities at work have also led to further integration and tolerance.

While there is still a long way to go and some issues may never be resolved, Belfast is buzzing. People enjoy the same lifestyle as those in the rest of the UK, working and playing hard, particularly now they can freely go out after work in the city centre to enjoy the new generation of restaurants, fringe theatre and bars, plus late-night shopping on a Thursday and drinking down the Golden Mile on a Friday. The cost of living is more or less the same as the rest of the UK, but you might find that bars, restaurants and hotels are cheaper than in London.

Most people are happy to show visitors round their city, but just be careful about being over pertinent about politics and religion, as it is a sensitive subject, and avoid wearing football shirts that might attract negative attention. Let them show you the murals or talk about their personal views and orientations if they like, otherwise take in the history at the museums and on the tour bus, and enjoy a large helping of the *craic* at the pub.

⬤ *Belfast pub culture is thriving*

Culture

The official language of the Republic of Ireland, the Irish language or Gaelic (*Gaeilge*), is recognised as their native language by a large percentage of the nationalist community. It's taught in Catholic schools as well as at the Gaelic language centre in the Falls Road, Cultúrlann MacAdam (see page 87). The church has traditionally been the hub of the community for Catholic residents and a unifying force through The Troubles. Today Mass attendance at Catholic churches has fallen to an all-time low in West Belfast, but there the church is still a regular meeting point for dance and music groups, where children (and adults) can learn traditional Irish dancing and how to play instruments heard in traditional Irish music, including the fiddle, mandolin, *bodhrán* and tin whistle. Gaelic football and hurling clubs are also affiliated round the church (see page 35). You often know when you're in a Catholic or Nationalist neighbourhood as many of the shop signs will be in Celtic script or even in Irish. You can see dancing on St Patrick's Day and in arts centres. The best place to hear traditional music is in pubs. Celtic art is shown in arts centres and the Gaelic language centre and you can buy it from the Wicker Man on High Street.

Other cultural forms have developed in spite of the turbulent past, particularly with the investment in arts centres and venues such as the Waterfront Hall (see page 69). Home to the Ulster Orchestra, it also stages classical music and operatic performances. Opera can also be seen outside Belfast at the **National Trust Castle Ward estate** in Strangford (❶ 028 4488 1204) during June, with productions by the specially formed Castle Ward Opera.

⬥ *The 2,250-seater auditorium at Waterfront Hall*

THE HAMELY TONGUE

As part of the Good Friday Agreement, it was agreed that 'respect and understanding and tolerance' would be given to the Ulster-Scots language. Also known as Ullans, Ulster-Scots is a variant of Scots that developed among the descendents of the Planters from Scotland since the 16th century and is spoken by an estimated 100,000 people in Northern Ireland. It was actually recognised as a language back in 1992. The Ulster Scots Agency promotes the study, development and use of the language and culture by publishing encouraging contemporary writing and providing teaching resources for schools. Speaking of the language has also meant a rise in other cultural forms associated with the Ulster Scots peoples, including music and literature. Many Ulster Scots events take place in Orange Halls. See the **Ulster Scots Agency** website (w www.ulsterscotsagency.com) for a list of upcoming events.

▶ *The Albert Clock and Custom House from the Lagan River*

Shopping

Belfast has plenty of opportunities for shopping and spending your hard-earned cash. The city centre is the main destination, with all the usual high-street stores along Donegall Place leading into Royal Avenue and the streets off it, especially Donegall Square North, Wellington Place, Upper Queen Street and Howard Street to the west, and Rosemary Street, Bridge Street, Castle Place, Cornmarket, Arthur Street, William Street and Ann Street to the east side. **Marks and Spencer** (☏ 028 9023 5235) can be found at the bottom of Donegall Place and **Dunnes Stores** (☏ 028 9032 2622) along Cornmarket.

The **Spires Mall** (☏ 028 9032 2284) on Wellington Street has a dozen or so shops, as does The Gallery (formerly Donegall Arcade, in Castle Place), which was refurbished and extended in 2008.

The **Victoria Square shopping centre** (☏ 028 9032 2277 ⓦ www.victoriasquare.com) opened in 2008 and is a showpiece with its glass dome and viewing platform, several new restaurants and a range of high-street and designer stores. **CastleCourt** (ⓐ Royal Avenue) remains a popular shopping centre, with more emphasis on high-street fashion and a choice of fast-food eateries.

Out of town, you'll find Marks and Spencer's third-largest store at **Sprucefield** (ⓦ www.sprucefieldcentre.co.uk), and factory outlets **Junction One** (ⓐ Off junction 1 of the M1 motorway) and **The Outlet** (ⓐ Banbridge on the A1), which opened in 2007. Both places offer all sorts of bargains, from clothes to home wares and toys.

There are plenty of places to buy gifts and souvenirs, but shop around. The in-house shops of all sorts of galleries are the place to go for those souvenirs for the people at work to which you wouldn't give a smidgeon of shelf space *chez vous*.

🔺 *The distinctive dome of the Victoria Square shopping centre*

Eating & drinking

There's little chance of avoiding an Ulster fry when you visit Belfast, although since it features mostly sausages, bacon and black or white pudding (along with soda bread, potato farls, fried eggs and sometimes mushrooms), vegetarians might be a bit put off. These days there are a few more vegetarian options, including plenty of cereals and some smoothie bars, but you'll need to shop around. Once you're set up with a good breakfast you'll not be wanting for anything for quite some time, and most locals usually grab a sandwich or light lunch. There are plenty of coffee shops and snack bars opening where you can have a doorstep sandwich, soup and wheaten bread or two-course lunch specials. Lunch is generally called 'dinner' and after work you go home for your 'tea', although plenty of people stay out in the city centre after work and there are lots of dining options.

In the restaurants you'll find traditional dishes such as Irish stew (once made from mutton but today from lamb, carrots and onions), sausage and champ (creamy mashed potato with scallions – spring onions), and boiled bacon (ham) and cabbage. There's usually plenty of meat on the menu, including succulent plates of Irish beef, pork and lamb. You also can't miss the fresh

PRICE CATEGORIES
Price ratings in this book are based on the average price of a two-course meal for one without drinks.
£ up to £15 ££ £15–25 £££ over £25

fish and seafood with warm bowls of seafood chowder and wheaten bread, fresh prawns, herrings, mackerel, lobster, oysters and mussels from the sea and freshwater fish such as salmon and trout. As you head up the Antrim Coast or south towards Strangford Lough and the Mournes, you'll find a greater selection of fish on the menu. Chinese and Italian restaurants have been popular in Belfast for decades, but the city's new positive image is attracting other international restaurants serving Japanese, Spanish and Indian cuisine.

Instead of spending a fortune in the restaurants you can also opt for a picnic, if the weather is good. Pick up some bread, cheese and ham from St George's Market (see page 70) and head out to the parks from City Hall and Ormeau Park in Botanic.

Bread plays an important part in the Belfast diet with potato bread (made from mashed potato), soda farls (raised with bicarbonate of soda rather than yeast), barm brack (fruit soda, a traditional bread to eat toasted on Halloween), boxty (made from potato, flour, egg and bicarb and said to have emerged during the potato famine), plain loaf (white sliced bread) and the good old crusty Belfast bap (bread roll). You'll see bread served with your Ulster fry, soups and chowder, in sandwiches and toasted with butter. The high level of milk production in Northern Ireland means plenty of dairy products from creamy fresh butter to strong hard cheese. Look out for locally produced goats' milk and cheese too – you'll be able to pick some up at St George's Market.

With all that bread you'll need to wash it down with a few drinks. Tea is very popular here, with buttered wheaten or toasted barm brack, and you'll want to try the famous Irish coffee, but in the end there's no excuse needed to head out for a few jars.

◓ *Apartment: one of the hippest eateries in town*

The most famous Irish drink is Guinness which is drunk plentifully in Belfast, but cider is also a popular drink. Armagh is known as the orchard county and you might pick up some homemade cider in the organic market, but in the pubs the cider is from the Republic of Ireland. Known as Bulmer's (not to be confused with the English Bulmer's) in the South, in Northern Ireland and the rest of the UK it is marketed as Magners. There has been a huge surge in sales in the past few years and you'll see plenty of large bottles (or draft) sold. Drink it in a pint glass with plenty of ice – they say it helps re-hydrate you! If that's not enough, finish with a few drams of Bushmills Irish Whiskey as a nightcap.

A RESTAURANT REVOLUTION

The development of the city centre has led to the evolution of a modern Irish cuisine, spearheaded by celebrity chefs such as Paul Rankin and Michael Deane. What makes the food modern is the variation on traditional dishes or an international twist with Asian, Mediterranean, Latin American or other influences in the ingredients. Expect crispy duck salad and roast hake in Parma ham from Rankin, and John Dory in crisped couscous or risotto of aged parmesan from Deane.

Entertainment & nightlife

Socialising plays a big part in Belfast life, from dinner and drinks to a full-on pub crawl, theatre and classical orchestras to traditional Irish music and fringe performing arts groups. There are no rules on where and when you should go out, except the licensing laws, although these too have relaxed in some areas, with some pubs staying open until midnight at the weekends and clubs until 02.00 or 03.00. Evening films usually start between 18.00 and 21.00, concerts and shows around 20.00 and gigs around 21.00.

At the Belfast Welcome Centre (see page 136) you can pick up a copy of *Whatabout*, which has listings for music and entertainment, pubs and clubs, theatre, opera and comedy, as well as family entertainment, shopping, eating and attractions. Also look out for a copy of *FATE*, which gives a round-up on the coolest bars, clubs, fashion and music.

For gentle, up-market bars, stay in the Cathedral Quarter, city centre and South Belfast, where hotel bars offer snacks and evening drinks, sometimes with music. There is a new crop of bars for the more mature and discerning crowd, including the likes of Café Vaudeville in Donegall Square South (see page 73). If you want something more down to earth, head to the Golden Mile, where pubs from Robinson's (see page 75) and the Crown Liquor Saloon (see page 74) down to Shaftesbury Square offer lively nights. Students and younger crowds also hang out in Botanic and Ormeau, where you'll find plenty of busy bars and pubs. The trendier crowd hang out in bars along the Lisburn Road. For clubbing, you're talking about much the same areas,

You're never far from a good pint in Belfast

● *Fibber Magee's hosts regular gigs*

along Ormeau Avenue, Botanic Avenue, Shaftesbury Square and Cathedral Quarter around Donegall Street. For gay bars, try Kremlin in Donegall Street (see page 75) and Mynt in Dunbar Street (see page 75), both in the Cathedral Quarter.

There's absolutely no shortage of music in Belfast, with something for everyone from traditional folk through to thrash metal, slash metal and nu rave. Just pick up the free listings magazines (see page 30) and see what inflates your Uilleann pipes. You can hear classical music and opera at the Waterfront Hall (see page 69), along with big-name concerts. The Ulster Orchestra and jazz groups play at the Ulster Hall in Bedford Street (see page 69). The best places to catch the very latest bands are The Limelight and Spring & Airbrake (see page 74). You can hear live traditional music in Fibber Magee's (see page 75), The John Hewitt (see page 74) and Cultúrlann MacAdam (see page 87), among others. During the warmer months there are open-air concerts outside the City Hall (see page 66), in Custom House Square and in Botanic Gardens.

Sadly, the only full-time producing theatre in Northern Ireland, the Lyric Theatre, has been demolished, but there are fringe centres such as Catalyst Arts (see page 68), Crescent Arts (see page 97) and Old Museum Arts Centre (see page 69), where you can see new artists and shows.

The Queen's Film Theatre (see page 98) shows a range of films in their original language with subtitles – screenings usually start between 18.00 and 21.00.

Your hotel should have a free booklet with the latest listings.

Sport & relaxation

SPECTATOR SPORTS

Football

The Carnegie Premier League is the main NI league but it doesn't carry the same prestige as the leagues in England, Scotland and the rest of Europe. One of Belfast's main teams is Linfield FC, based at **Windsor Park** (ⓐ Windsor Park, Donegall Avenue) which is also the venue for the Northern Ireland team's international matches.

Carnegie Premier League ⓦ http://irishpremierleague.com
Irish Football Association ⓦ www.irishfa.com

⬤ *Catch great rugby at Ravenshill*

Gaelic Football

Gaelic football, a cross between football, rugby and war, is hugely popular among the Catholic community, with teams affiliated to church parishes. County Antrim trains and holds its home games at **Casement Park** (☎ 028 9060 5868) in the Falls Road. It's not a game for delicate blossoms and is very entertaining to watch.

Horseracing

Northern Ireland's premier racecourse is **Down Royal Racecourse** (🏠 24 Ballyduggan Road, Downpatrick 🌐 www.downroyal.com) at Downpatrick. There are regular fixtures throughout the year and tickets are available online.

Hurling

As with Gaelic Football, Belfast's hurling teams are affiliated to the local parishes. Once again, Casement Park is the venue for the County Antrim team's home games.

Ice Hockey

The **Belfast Giants** (🌐 www.belfastgiants.co.uk) are the major team in the city and their base is at the **Odyssey Arena** (🏠 Odyssey Arena, Queen's Quay ☎ 028 9703 9074 🌐 www.odysseyarena.com), where the home Elite League games are played against other UK teams.

Rugby

Ravenhill Stadium (🏠 Ravenhill Stadium, Ravenhill) is home to **Ulster Rugby** (🌐 www.ulsterrugby.ie), which has stayed in the Irish Rugby Football Union since partition in 1921, meaning six of the nine counties of the Ulster branch are in Northern Ireland

and three are in the Republic of Ireland. So you can expect to see games against Leinster, Munster and Connacht, as well as teams from Scotland, England and Wales.

PARTICIPATION SPORTS

Belfast has numerous sports centres run by the city council, as well as private gyms and health clubs, including **Fitness First** (ⓦ www.fitnessfirst.co.uk), **LA Fitness** (ⓦ www.lafitness.co.uk) and **LivingWell Health Club** (ⓦ www.livingwell.com).

Golf

Northern Ireland is a popular destination for golf and there are several courses within easy reach of Belfast, including **Hilton Templepatrick Golf Club** (ⓦ www.hilton.co.uk/templepatrick), **Royal Belfast Golf Club** in Holywood (ⓦ www.royalbelfast.com) and **Royal County Down** in Newcastle (ⓦ www.royalcountydown.org).

Outdoors and adventure sports

Close to Belfast you can go walking in **Colin Glen Forest Park** (ⓦ www.colinglentrust.org), along the Lagan Towpath to Lisburn (see page 91) or in Cave Hill Country Park (see page 82). For longer treks head to the Glens of Antrim (see page 121) or the Mourne Mountains (see page 110). In the Mournes you can also go climbing and orienteering, with courses at **Tollymore Mountain Centre** (ⓦ www.tollymore.com). **Bluelough Adventure Centre** (ⓦ www.mountainandwater.com) runs adventure days plus courses and practice days in canoeing, climbing, bouldering, camp craft, mountain biking and much more .

Accommodation

In general, accommodation in Belfast costs around the same as in other parts of the UK, but there's quite a variety of places to stay, and with the city's booming development, new hotels are opening quite regularly. It's best to book somewhere in advance. The tourist office website has a 'special deals' section as well as full listings of other accommodation according to classification, Ⓦ www.gotobelfast.com. Also try the **Northern Ireland Tourist Board** (Ⓦ www.visitnorthernireland.com) and **Tourism Ireland** (Ⓦ www.discoverireland.com). There are several websites offering online bookings, often with discounts; some of the best include Ⓦ www.goireland.com, www.expedia.co.uk, www.hotels.co.uk, www.opodo.co.uk and www.hini.org.uk

If you find yourself in Belfast without anywhere to stay, the staff in the Belfast Welcome Centre in Donegall Place are very helpful. Alternatively, try some of the suggestions below according to your taste and budget.

The best places to stay are in the city centre along the streets around Donegall Square, along Great Victoria Street to Shaftesbury Square, Botanic, Stranmillis and Malone in South Belfast. There are some large hotels such as the Hilton, by the Waterfront Hall,

PRICE CATEGORIES
Gradings used in this book are based on the average price for a double room per night, including breakfast.
£ up to £60   ££ £60–100   £££ over £100

and the Radisson in the old Gasworks south of St George's Market, and new places are opening in the Cathedral Quarter. You can find places to stay in other parts of Belfast, including along the Antrim Road in North Belfast, Dunmurry in West Belfast and Stormont in East Belfast, but for easy access to attractions it's easier and safer to stay more centrally. For out-of-town options, see the relevant chapters or the websites on the previous page.

HOTELS

Travelodge Belfast Central £ Reasonably priced hotel with a breakfast option, located within crawling distance of Fibber Magee's and other lively pubs. ⓐ 15 Brunswick Street (City Centre) ⓣ 0870 191 1687 ⓦ www.travelodge.co.uk ⓝ Bus: Europa Buscentre

Benedict's ££ Located at the top end of Belfast's Golden Mile, this trendy hotel has a gothic themed bar, live DJs and music, and slick guestrooms in modern décor. ⓐ 7–21 Bradbury Place, Shaftesbury Square (City Centre) ⓣ 028 9059 1999 ⓦ www.benedictshotel.co.uk ⓝ Bus: 8A, 7B

Days Hotel ££ Northern Ireland's largest hotel, with spacious and comfortable guestrooms. Located just off the Golden Mile near Europa Buscentre. ⓐ 40 Hope Street (City Centre) ⓣ 028 9024 2494 ⓦ www.dayshotelbelfast.co.uk ⓝ Bus: Europa Buscentre, Train: Great Victoria Street

Holiday Inn Belfast ££ Located in the heart of Belfast's Golden Mile with contemporary rooms, restaurant and bar. ⓐ 22 Ormeau

Avenue (City Centre) ☎ 0870 400 9005 🅕 028 9062 6546
Ⓦ www.ichotelsgroup.com Ⓝ Train: Great Victoria Street

Madison's ££ Stylish small hotel with bar, restaurant and club, this is a favourite with rock bands and is located in the heart of lively Botanic. Ⓐ 59–63 Botanic Avenue (City Centre) ☎ 028 9050 9800 Ⓦ www.madisonshotel.com Ⓝ Bus: 7A-B, 8A-B

🔺 *The Europa Hotel: in the heart of the city*

Stormont Hotel ££ Overlooks the Northern Ireland government grounds and has two restaurants. ⓐ Upper Newtownards Road (South & East Belfast) ⓣ 028 9027 1066 ⓦ www.hastingshotels.com ⓝ Bus: 20A

The Crescent Townhouse Hotel £££ Intimate and stylish hotel located in the heart of the cool Botanic area, with canopy beds and Victorian-style roll-top baths, plus a brasserie and bar. ⓐ 13 Lower Crescent (City Centre) ⓣ 028 9032 3349 ⓦ www.crescenttownhouse.com ⓝ Bus: 7

Europa Hotel £££ Renowned as 'the most bombed hotel in Europe', but don't worry – that dates back to The Troubles. It remains one of the best hotels in the city, located next to the Grand Opera House and opposite the Crown Liquor Saloon. ⓐ Great Victoria Street (City Centre) ⓣ 028 9027 1066 ⓕ 028 9032 7800 ⓦ www.hastingshotels.com ⓝ Bus: Europa Buscentre

Hilton Belfast £££ Located next to the Waterfront Hall, this 5-star hotel has restaurants, bars, riverside views and a health club. ⓐ 4 Lanyon Place (City Centre) ⓣ 028 9027 7000 ⓕ 028 9027 7277 ⓦ www.hilton.co.uk/belfast ⓔ reservations.belfast@hilton.com ⓝ Bus: Laganside Buscentre

Malmaison £££ You'll find stylish and slinky guestrooms here or large suites named after the cranes that helped build the *Titanic*. The hotel also has a brasserie, bar and a gym. ⓐ 34–38 Victoria Street (City Centre) ⓣ 028 9022 0200 ⓦ www.malmaison-belfast.com ⓔ belfast@malmaison.com ⓝ Bus: Donegall Square/Royal Avenue

The Merchant Hotel £££ This swanky hotel was once the headquarters of The Ulster Bank; the 19th-century building has been transformed to include luxury accommodation. You can also pop in for traditional afternoon tea, dinner and drinks. ⓐ 35–39 Waring Street (City Centre) ⓣ 028 9023 4888 ⓦ www.themerchanthotel.com ⓝ Bus: Laganside Bus Centre

Radisson SAS Hotel Belfast £££ Modern, comfortable hotel with restaurant, bar and large car park. ⓐ The Gasworks, Cromac Place (City Centre) ⓣ 028 9043 4065 ⓦ www.radisson.com ⓝ Bus: 77, 30

Ten Square £££ Chic, central boutique hotel with Asian-style guestrooms, low-level beds and rich cream carpets. ⓐ 10 Donegall Square South (City Centre) ⓣ 028 9024 1001 ⓦ www.tensquare.co.uk ⓔ reservations@tensquare.co.uk ⓝ Bus: Donegall Square

YOUTH HOSTELS

Arnies Backpackers £ Located near Queen's University, you'll be near all the nightlife and won't have to pay a packet. ⓐ 63 Fitzwilliam Street (South & East Belfast) ⓣ 028 9024 2867 ⓦ www.arniesbackpackers.co.uk ⓝ Bus: 8A-B

Belfast International Youth Hostel £ Located right on Belfast's Golden Mile, this hostel is well located for sightseeing and going out. ⓐ 22–32 Donegall Road (City Centre) ⓣ 028 9031 5435 ⓦ www.hini.org.uk ⓝ Bus: 8A, 7B

THE BEST OF BELFAST

There's a lot to see and do in Belfast but if you've only got a few hours or days to spare, try some of the following must-sees.

TOP 10 ATTRACTIONS

- **Belfast Citysightseeing bus tour** A good introduction to Belfast, covering the city centre and nearby attractions (see page 65)

- **City Hall** The city centre's most prominent landmark: see the elaborate interior or picnic in the gardens (see page 66)

- **Ulster Museum** A treasure trove of history, science and art, giving a thorough insight into Northern Ireland's past and present (see page 99)

- **Crown Liquor Saloon** One of the oldest and most elaborate bars in the city – sit in a 'snug' with a pint of Guinness (see page 74)

The opulent Crown Liquor Saloon

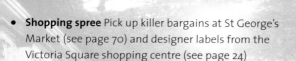

- **Shopping spree** Pick up killer bargains at St George's Market (see page 70) and designer labels from the Victoria Square shopping centre (see page 24)

- **Concert at Waterfront Hall** Belfast's primary concert hall hosts the Ulster Orchestra plus opera and comedy (see page 69)

- **West Belfast Murals** Take a guided tour or take in the political murals at your own pace (see pages 86–7)

- **Belfast Titanic Trail** Hear anecdotes about the city centre from the City Hall and Albert Clock to the Titanic (see page 90)

- **W5 at Odyssey** An interactive discovery centre with scientific experiments, creative challenges and feats of physical strength (see page 94)

- **Hit the town** Bar hop down the Golden Mile – start in the city centre and head towards Shaftesbury Square and Botanic (see pages 72–5)

Suggested itineraries

HALF-DAY: BELFAST IN A HURRY

If you've only a few hours free, hop on a Belfast Citysightseeing bus tour (see page 65). In 90 minutes you'll get a flavour of the city centre, Cathedral Quarter (see page 65), Titanic Quarter (see page 96), West Belfast Murals (see page 86), University District (see page 90) and Golden Mile/nightlife (see page 30). If you've time left, jump off at the Europa Hotel (see page 40) and cross the road to the Crown Liquor Saloon (see page 74) for a pint.

1 DAY: TIME TO SEE A LITTLE MORE

If you've got a whole day, load up on a carb-tastic Ulster fry then take the bus tour in the morning, stop for lunch in the Crown Liquor Saloon (see page 74) and then explore the city centre on foot. Take a free tour round City Hall (see page 66) and take a peek at the rich collection of Irish books in the Linen Hall (see page 68). If you've time, have a little wander up Royal Avenue to buy some souvenirs in the Belfast Welcome Centre (see page 136).

2–3 DAYS: TIME TO SEE MUCH MORE

Lucky you: this means you've got time to explore beyond the city centre. Depending on your interests, you can pursue one of the above suggestions in depth. An alternative idea is to take a Titanic Boat Tour (see page 96), which tells the story of the ill-fated vessel's tragically short life (don't worry: there's no iceberg). If the weather is good, why not spend the day out of town at the Ulster Folk & Transport Museum (see page 112)? There should also be time for an afternoon's intensive shopping along Royal Avenue and at the Victoria Square shopping centre (see page 24) and a night out at the Café Vaudeville (see page 73) for jazz and cocktails; alternatively, whooping it up at Fibber Magee's (see page 75) will give you a blast of some traditional Irish music; Botanic Avenue is the place to go for a more studenty vibe.

LONGER: ENJOYING BELFAST TO THE FULL

If you've more than a couple of days on your hands, expose yourself to the glory of the countryside and drive or book an organised tour outside the city. Some of the best days out include a motorised poodle along the stunning Antrim Coast to Giant's Causeway (see page 119) and Bushmills Distillery (see page 117). Another sublimely seductive notion would be a day in Downpatrick visiting the Cathedral (see page 105), Down County Museum (see page 108) or going for a bracing walk in the Mourne Mountains (see page 110) and a fish supper in Newcastle (see page 111). Viva Belfast!

● Bus tours take in all the sights

Something for nothing

You don't have to spend a fortune getting to know Belfast as there are plenty of free or fairly cheap activities to keep you occupied. Your first stop should be the Belfast Welcome Centre (see page 136) where information, advice, maps and brochures are all free.

Start by exploring the city centre on foot. Tours of City Hall (see page 66) and browsing the superb collection of books at the Linen Hall Library (see page 68) don't cost a penny. Take in top attractions such as the Albert Clock, Custom House Square, Lagan Lookout, Europa Hotel, Grand Opera House and Crown Liquor Saloon (see pages 60–75). Then head south along Victoria Street to see the impressive Queen's University (see page 95) and on to the Ulster Museum (see page 99).

If you're good on your feet head up the Falls Road and spend some time looking at the numerous political murals that adorn the houses there. These beautifully executed – but, not surprisingly, rather visceral – expressions of socio-political feeling are a reminder of the sectarian divisions that came so close to destroying the city.

Next, pop into Cultúrlann MacAdam, the Irish language and culture centre, where you can stop for a café lunch, hear locals speaking Gaelic and have a browse in the bookshop (see page 87). Don't get carried away by the warmth of the welcome and the heady magnetism of the culture: this is not the place to debut your tribute to *Riverdance* in the hope of securing investment.

On a good day, walk or cycle along the Lagan towpath, which runs 10 miles from Stranmillis in South Belfast to Lisburn in County

Down (see page 91). The route runs along the riverbank through beautiful scenery, urban parkland and nature trails. If that's too far, then head for one of the city parks, including Botanic Gardens for its impressive plant collections and relaxing lawns (see page 91), Cave Hill Country Park for Belfast Castle and panoramic city views (see page 82), the Japanese Garden at Sir Thomas and Lady Dixon Park or Ormeau Park for woodland and wildlife (see page 95).

⬤ *The Linen Hall Library: fascinating and free*

When it rains

The likelihood of it raining when you're in Belfast is quite high, so you should really just take a raincoat and an umbrella and not let a few drops of rain stop you from enjoying the sights outdoors. The open-top buses are swapped for ones with roofs on rainy days, so you can still take a tour round the city. The same goes for black taxi tours, but if you really want to get out of the rain, there's no shortage of options.

Take a tour round City Hall (see page 66), which will last about an hour, and takes in the grand staircase, oak council chamber, the ornate dome and other features of this Classical Renaissance building. You can spend several hours in the Ulster Museum (see page 99), which has something for everyone including art, archaeology, local history and natural science, plus special exhibitions.

The Odyssey (see pages 94–5) is a fantastic all-day option (especially good if you have children with you) and you can park the car there if you have one. Spend the morning getting hands-on in W5, an interactive centre of discovery, then have lunch in the Odyssey Pavilion before seeing a film at the IMAX cinema in the afternoon. You might even be able to catch a game by the Belfast Giants ice hockey team (see page 35), if you're really lucky.

There are several indoor shopping options, including the showpiece Victoria Square shopping centre and the older CastleCourt Shopping Centre (see page 24), where you've everything you need to keep you fed, watered and clothed for the day.

If the rain carries on into the evening, take in a film at the Queen's Film Theatre (see page 98), classical music at the Waterfront Hall (see page 69) or performing arts at the Crescent Arts Centre (see page 97). Of course you could also take refuge in one of the city's many public houses, where the company's so convivial that you might be tempted to knock out a quick rain dance to keep the party going.

◯ *CastleCourt Shopping Centre: no umbrella needed*

On arrival

TIME DIFFERENCE

Belfast follows Greenwich Mean Time (GMT). During Daylight Saving Time (last Sunday in March to last Sunday in October), the clocks are put ahead 1 hour – British Summer Time (BST).

ARRIVING

By air

Belfast has two airports: Belfast International Airport and George Best Belfast City Airport. The international airport is located 13 km (8 miles) northwest of the city and is Northern Ireland's busiest airport. Facilities include shops and restaurants, bureaux de change, postal services, cash machines, airport information, Business Lounge and baby changing facilities.

The blue and white Airport Express 300 bus operates between the airport and Belfast every 10–20 minutes and leaves from the bus stop opposite the terminal exit. The bus stops at Laganside Buscentre and Europa Buscentre (approximate journey time 30–40 minutes, depending on traffic). There are also approved taxis available outside the terminal.

George Best Belfast City Airport is between Belfast and Holywood, five miles from the city centre. There are two shops and a range of restaurants/snack bars, as well as cash dispensers, bureaux de change and wireless internet access.

A shuttle bus operates between the airport and the Sydenham railway station. Translink operates a twice-hourly rail service to Belfast Central, Botanic and Great Victoria Street stations (journey time up to 15 minutes). Flexibus operates the Airport Express

⬤ *Buses connect both airports to the city*

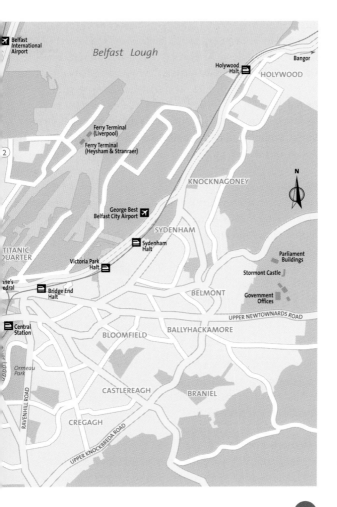

bus service (route 600) every 20 minutes from the airport
terminal to Belfast Europa Bus Centre, which takes 13 minutes.
Belfast International Airport Ⓦ www.belfastairport.com
George Best Belfast City Airport Ⓦ www.belfastcityairport.com

By rail

Belfast railway stations include **Belfast Central**, **Great Victoria
Street**, **Botanic** and **City Hospital** (see Ⓦ www.translink.co.uk for
details of all).

By road

Long-distance buses arrive at **Europa Buscentre** (ⓐ Glengall
Street), which leads on to Great Victoria Street, next to the
Europa Hotel and just a few minutes' walk from Donegall
Square and City Hall.

Visitors arriving by car at Belfast ferry port should follow
signs for the A2, M3 or Belfast city centre. From Larne ferry port
head for the A8, then M2 and A2. From north and northwest
you'll arrive via the M2, from the south via the M1 or A1.

By water

There is a ferry port in Belfast, close to the city centre. It moved
to a new terminal building two miles along the north side of
Belfast Lough in 2008, so you'll need to take bus number 96
from the city centre to Westbank Road or get a taxi.

FINDING YOUR FEET

Visitors to Belfast will be greeted with a warm Northern Irish
welcome and the locals are keen to show that the city has a lot

to offer. People are generally easy-going and it won't be difficult
to quickly immerse yourself into the *craic* (good time). It isn't
a large city, so even if you wander down a side street in the city
centre, it won't be long before you find your way back to a main
road. If you do get lost, just ask for directions – you'll find that
people are willing to help.

ORIENTATION

Belfast city centre is bound by the Westlink (which links the M2
and the M1) to the north and west, by the M2 and River Lagan
to the east, and Shaftesbury Square to the south. At the heart
of the city centre is Donegall Square with the landmark City
Hall (see page 66) at its centre. North of Donegall Square are
the main shopping streets of Donegall Place, Royal Avenue,
High Street and Cornmarket and the oldest parts of the city.
The Cathedral Quarter is located at the northern end of the
city centre around Donegall Street. Heading east, High Street
crosses Victoria Street and leads to the Albert Clock, Custom
House Square and the River Lagan. To the south along the river
is the Lagan Lookout (see pages 91 & 94), the Waterfront Hall
(see page 60) and Central Station.

GETTING AROUND

Visitors can easily walk around the city centre on foot, and
even south to the Ulster Museum (see page 99), west along
Falls and Shankill roads, or along the riverfront. However, for
longer distances or if you're tired, there is an efficient urban bus
service which is called the Metro, with main departure points in
Donegall Square and Wellington Place. You can buy Metro day

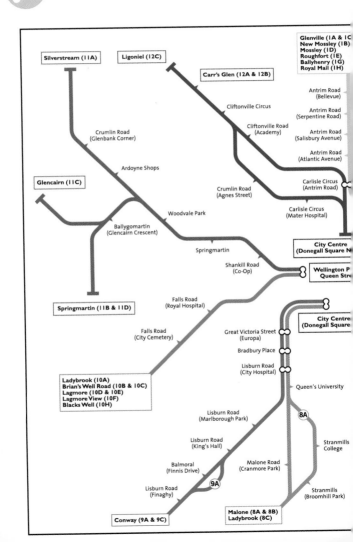

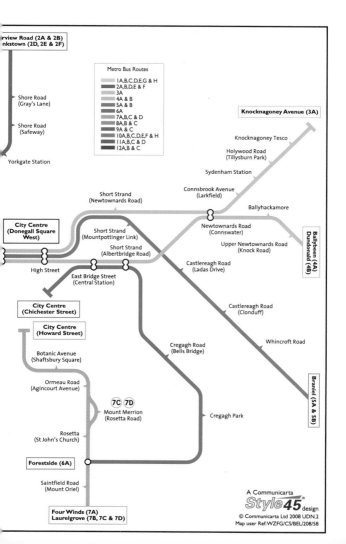

rview Road (2A & 2B)
nkstown (2D, 2E & 2F)

Shore Road
(Gray's Lane)

Shore Road
(Safeway)

Yorkgate Station

Metro Bus Routes

1A,B,C,D,E,G & H
2A,B,D,E & F
3A
4A & B
5A & B
6A
7A,B,C & D
8A,B & C
9A & C
10A,B,C,D,E,F & H
11A,B,C & D
12A,B & C

Knocknagoney Avenue (3A)

Knocknagoney Tesco

Holywood Road
(Tillysburn Park)

Sydenham Station

Connsbrook Avenue
(Larkfield)

Short Strand
(Newtownards Road)

Ballyhackamore

**City Centre
(Donegall Square
West)**

Short Strand
(Mountpottinger Link)

Newtownards Road
(Connswater)

Short Strand
(Albertbridge Road)

Upper Newtownards Road
(Knock Road)

High Street

Castlereagh Road
(Ladas Drive)

**Ballybeen (4A)
Dundonald (4B)**

East Bridge Street
(Central Station)

Castlereagh Road
(Clonduff)

**City Centre
(Chichester Street)**

**City Centre
(Howard Street)**

Whincroft Road

Botanic Avenue
(Shaftsbury Square)

Cregagh Road
(Bells Bridge)

Braniel (5A & 5B)

Ormeau Road
(Agincourt Avenue)

7C 7D
Mount Merrion
(Rosetta Road)

Rosetta
(St John's Church)

Cregagh Park

Forestside (6A)

Saintfield Road
(Mount Oriel)

**Four Winds (7A)
Laurelgrove (7B, 7C & 7D)**

A Communicarta
Style 45 design
© Communicarta Ltd 2008 UDN.2
Map user Ref:WZFG/CS/BEL/208/58

tickets, giving you the freedom to hop on and off buses as you please. You can buy these from the driver or from the Metro Ticket and Information kiosk in Donegall Square West.

Alternatively, there are shared black taxis that charge a similar rate to buses, operating from Bedford Street (off High Street) to the Shankill Road or from the car park on the corner of Castle Street and King Street. To get further afield, buses from Laganside Buscentre go to North Down, while Europa Buscentre serves the rest of the province, Dublin and international destinations.

CAR HIRE

If you're only planning on staying in Belfast, you don't really need to hire a car. However, if you want to get around outside the city as you please, then car hire is available at both Belfast International Airport and George Best Belfast City Airport:

Avis ❶ International Airport 0870 608 6316,
City Airport 0870 608 6317 ❿ www.avis.co.uk

Budget ❶ International & City Airports 0844 444 0002
(customer services), 0844 581 2231 (reservations) ❿ www.budget.ie

Europcar ❶ International & City Airports 028 9045 0904
❿ www.europcar.co.uk

Hertz ❶ International Airport 028 9073 2541,
City Airport 028 9073 9400 ❿ www.hertz.co.uk

National Car Rental ❶ International & City Airports 028 9073 9400
❿ www.nationalcar.co.uk

❶ City Hall

THE CITY OF
Belfast

City Centre

The oldest part of Belfast is High Street and Castle Place, where the city's first castle once stood. Off here you'll discover various 'entries', side alleys with historic pubs and bars hidden away, and at the end the iconic Albert Memorial Clock. Just north of here is the artsy Cathedral Quarter, around Donegall Street, with St Anne's Cathedral at its centre. Today the heart of the city has shifted south to Donegall Square, where City Hall marks Belfast's city status.

SIGHTS & ATTRACTIONS

Albert Memorial Clock

Built between 1865–70 as a memorial to Queen Victoria's late consort, the Albert Memorial Clock is now one of the city's primary landmarks, partly because of its distinctive lean of around 1.4 m (4½ ft), blamed on the fact that it was built on reclaimed land. Constructed in 1865 from sandstone, and standing over 34 m (111 ft) high, the clock has a life-size statue of Prince Albert on the west side and a 2-tonne bell.
ⓐ Victoria Street ⓝ Bus: Laganside Buscentre

Belfast Cathedral

Also known as The Cathedral Church of St Anne (or St Anne's Cathedral), this was Belfast's first Church of Ireland parish. The first foundation stone was laid in 1899 but it wasn't completed until 1981. In 2007, a new modern, stainless steel spire was erected, which towers above the cathedral and is

⬥ *The Albert Memorial Clock*

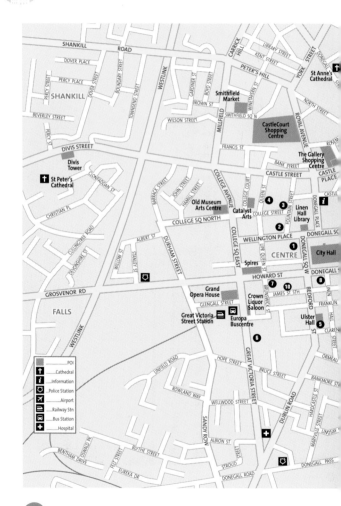

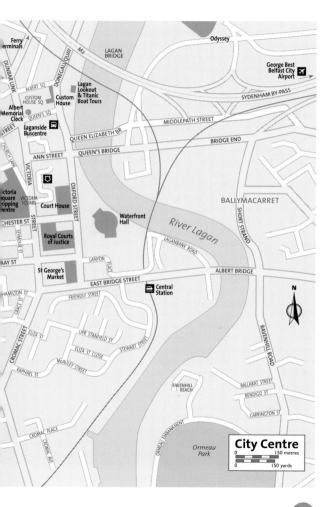

Ferry Terminals

DUNBAR LINK

DONEGALL QUAY

M2

LAGAN BRIDGE

Odyssey

George Best Belfast City Airport

SYDENHAM BY-PASS

ALBERT SQ

CUSTOM HOUSE SQ

Custom House

Lagan Lookout & Titanic Boat Tours

Albert Memorial Clock

QUEEN'S SQ

MIDDLEPATH STREET

STREET

Laganside Buscentre

QUEEN ELIZABETH BR

BRIDGE END

CHURCH LANE

ANN STREET

QUEEN'S BRIDGE

VICTORIA

ctoria quare opping entre

VICTORIA SQUARE

BALLYMACARRET

CHESTER ST

STREET

Court House

OXFORD STREET

Waterfront Hall

River Lagan

SHORT STRAND

SCHOOL ST

Royal Courts of Justice

LAGANBANK ROAD

MAY ST

LANYON PLACE

ALBERT BRIDGE

N

St George's Market

EAST BRIDGE STREET

HAMILTON ST

GRACE ST

FRIENDLY STREET

Central Station

RAVENHILL ROAD

CROMAC STREET

ELIZA ST

UPR STANFIELD ST

ELIZA ST CLOSE

STEWART STREET

McAULEY STREET

RAPHAEL ST

RAVENHILL REACH

BALLARAT STREET

BENDIGO ST

CARRINGTON ST

CROMAC PLACE

CROMAC AVE

ORMEAU EMBANKMENT

Ormeau Park

City Centre

0 _____ 150 metres

0 _____ 150 yards

○ *Belfast Cathedral*

lit up at night. ⓐ Lower Donegall Street ⓣ 028 9032 8332
ⓦ www.belfastcathedral.org ⓛ 10.00–16.00 Mon–Sat
ⓝ Bus: Royal Avenue

Belfast Citysightseeing bus tour

The quickest way to get a flavour of the city, buses leave at regular
intervals from Castle Place and follow a circular route taking in
Belfast city centre, Cathedral Quarter, Titanic Quarter, Stormont,
Laganside, Crumlin Road Courthouse and Gaol, Shankill Road, Peace
Line, Falls Road, University District and Botanic nightlife areas.
You're given a route map on the bus and there is a live commentary
by a local guide on the way. You can hop on and off *en route*.
ⓐ Castle Place ⓣ 028 9045 9035 ⓦ www.belfastcitysightseeing.com
ⓛ 10.00–16.00 (tours every 45 mins) Sept–May; 09.30-16.30
(tours every 30 mins) June–Aug ⓝ Bus: Royal Avenue, Donegall
Square. Admission charge

Cathedral Quarter

One of the oldest city districts, the Cathedral Quarter had become
quite run down, but it's now seeing something of a renaissance.
The main focal point is Belfast Cathedral (see page 60) on
Donegall Street and the roads and alleys around it. A favourite
with artists and musicians, theatre groups and dance studios
due to the low rents, it is fast becoming a trendy arts/media area
with new companies moving in and restorations taking place.
Look out for the Duke of York pub (see page 74), the original
premises of the Northern Bank, Irish News, News Letter and
St Patrick's Church, as well as community arts centres and
galleries. ⓐ Donegall Street ⓝ Bus: Royal Avenue

City Hall

Built in the Edwardian baroque style – and, indeed, thought
to be the finest example of that genre – and opened in 1906,
City Hall stands on the site of the old White Linen Hall. Plans
for the building began after Queen Victoria, in a fit of generosity,
gave Belfast city status in 1888, in recognition of the contribution
that its residents' blood, sweat and tears made to the Empire's
coffers. There was clearly no great rush to get things moving,
however, as construction only began ten years later under the
magnificently named architect, Sir Alfred Brumwell Thomas.
Highlights include the emphatic grand entrance, the main
dome with its whispering gallery, grand staircase and the
mural by Belfast artist John Luke. City Hall is one of Belfast's
leading chilling out locations. The ample grounds are popular
with office workers who want to enjoy their lunch break in
the sun. The front gates meanwhile are a major hangout for
Goths, emos, bikers and anyone else looking for a meeting
place and a natter. City Hall is closed for renovation until
mid-2009 so phone to check if you plan to visit before then.
ⓐ Donegall Square ⓣ 028 9032 0202, minicom 028 9027 0405
ⓦ www.belfastcity.gov.uk ⓛ 09.00–17.00 Mon–Fri ⓑ Bus:
Donegall Square

Crown Liquor Saloon

A popular venue with locals and tourists, this is a fine example of a
Victorian public house or 'gin palace', now owned by the National
Trust. The outside is clad in colourful tiles, while the inside is a
rich mix of carved wooden snugs, red granite-top bars, mosaics,
tiles, mirrors and columns, all cleaned and renovated in 2007.

A RIGHT ROYAL MONIKER

An old Belfast story has it that the name of the Crown Liquor Saloon was chosen by the Protestant wife of the landlord to show her allegiance to the British monarchy. Her husband, a Catholic, wasn't keen on this idea, and only agreed if he could put a mosaic of a crown in the doorway – that way everyone would have to step on it as they walked in to the pub. The mosaic, together with the Crown's celebrated Victorian snugs (complete with antique bells for getting the attention of the bar staff), is still there to greet visitors today.

ⓐ 46 Great Victoria Street ⓣ 028 9027 9901 ⓦ www.crownbar.com
ⓝ Bus: Europa Buscentre, Donegall Square

Custom House Square

Renovated a few years ago to highlight its original use as a speakers' corner, the paved square now has a bronze statue of 'The Speaker' and large copper-based lights along its edge representing 'The Hecklers'. The historic Calder Fountain was also restored, and lights follow the course of the underground River Farset (which runs the length of High Street). The square is now used for concerts, festivals and other events as well as being a favourite hangout for skateboarders. The central focus of the square is the mid-19th-century Custom House, one of the few remaining Custom Houses in the UK still occupied by Her Majesty's Revenue and Customs Officers. It is open to the public on European Heritage Open Days only. ⓐ Custom House Square ⓝ Bus: Laganside Buscentre

CULTURE

Catalyst Arts

One of the city's fringe arts centres, this artist-run venue supports innovative projects in art, film, photography, music and literature. ⓐ 2nd Floor, 5 College Court ⓣ 028 9031 3303 ⓦ www.catalystarts.org.uk ⓔ info@catalystarts.org.uk ⓛ Performance times vary – check website for details ⓝ Bus: Donegall Square/Royal Avenue. Admission charge

Grand Opera House

You're unlikely to see opera at this historic venue but you can catch off-West End theatre, musicals and pantomimes. The renovated opera house now has an extension that has added an all-day café/bistro, bars and more wheelchair space and access. ⓐ Great Victoria Street ⓣ 028 9024 1919 ⓦ www.goh.co.uk ⓛ Various ⓝ Bus: Europa Buscentre/Donegall Square

Linen Hall Library

Founded in 1788, the Linen Hall contains the best Irish and Local Studies Collection of books covering everything from early Belfast and Ulster to the contemporary NI Political Collection on The Troubles. A centre of cultural and creative life, it hosts a varied programme of exhibitions, readings, discussion groups and lectures. Use the library for reference or read a few of your favourite newspapers. ⓐ 17 Donegall Square North ⓣ 028 9032 1707 ⓦ www.linenhall.com ⓛ 09.30–17.30 Mon–Fri, 09.30–13.00 Sat; closed for one week in July, check website for details ⓝ Bus: Donegall Square

Old Museum Arts Centre

Presents contemporary theatre, music, dance and visual art from Northern Ireland and overseas. Plans are underway to build a state-of-the-art replacement in the Cathedral Quarter. ⓐ 7 College Square North ⓣ 028 9023 5053 ⓦ www.oldmuseumartscentre.org ⓛ Performance times vary – check website for details ⓝ Donegall Square. Admission charge

Ulster Hall

You can see theatre, classical concerts, jazz and popular music in this venue, which is closed for renovation until late 2009. ⓐ Bedford Street ⓣ 028 9032 3900 ⓦ www.ulsterhall.co.uk ⓛ Performance times vary – check website for details ⓝ Bus: Donegall Square

Waterfront Hall

The city's major concert and conference venue. ⓐ 2 Lanyon Place ⓣ 028 9033 4455 ⓦ www.waterfront.co.uk ⓛ Performance times vary – check website for details ⓝ Bus: Laganside Bus Station. Admission charge

RETAIL THERAPY

The hub of Belfast's shopping is around Donegall Place and Royal Avenue, where you'll find high-street stores and the large CastleCourt shopping centre (see page 24). More shops can be found along High Street and Cornmarket, which leads to Belfast's new showpiece Victoria Square shopping centre (see page 24). Home to high-street and designer stores, it also boasts several

MARKETS

The main market in Belfast city centre is **St George's Market** on Oxford Street/May Street. It's a late 19th-century market that's had a makeover, buffing up its Victorian splendour. On Friday there's a vibrant mixed market (🕐 06.00–13.00) and on Saturday jazz and food at the City Food & Garden Market (🕐 10.00–16.00). Catch the free market bus on market days from Donegall Place or Castle Place.

Smithfield Market was once a thriving market but the old Victorian building was sadly demolished in 1974. After years of pre-fabricated units, a new market building opened in 1986. It's not as trendy as St George's but sells a little of everything and is useful for products and trades no longer found on the high street, including leather workers, a seamstress and martial arts products (🕐 09.00–17.00 Mon–Sat).

restaurants, a cinema and a glass dome with a viewing platform. The Gallery (see page 24) is another small shopping centre.

TAKING A BREAK

Apartment £ ❶ Trendy café-bar-restaurant with panini and pasta downstairs and Asian-fusion dining upstairs; and then there are the views of City Hall. ⓐ 2 Donegall Square West ☏ 028 9050 9777 ⓦ www.apartmentbelfast.com 🕐 09.00–01.00 (last food orders 21.00) Mon–Sat, 12.00–01.00 (last food orders 20.00) Sun

La Boca £ ❷ An Argentine restaurant in Belfast, no less (and an art gallery, too). Top dishes to try in this chic and friendly eaterie are bruschetta of roast red pepper and olive tapenade and ensalada verde. The wine list is fabulous. **ⓐ** 6 Fountain Street **❶** 028 9032 3087 **Ⓦ** www.labocabelfast.com **⏰** 11.30–23.00 Mon–Sat, 11.30–22.30 Sun

Café Paul Rankin £ ❸ Owned by TV chef Paul Rankin, this café serves deli sandwiches, soups and salads. There's also a branch in CastleCourt shopping centre. **ⓐ** 29 Fountain Street **❶** 028 9031 5090 **Ⓦ** www.rankingroup.co.uk **⏰** 07.30–17.30 Mon–Wed, Fri & Sat, 07.30–19.00 Thur, 13.00–17.00 Sun

⬥ *Hit St George's Market at dawn on Friday*

Café Renoir £ ❹ Try homemade scones, fresh bread and organic jams from the Loney family farm. The triple club sandwich is particularly popular. ⓐ 5–7 Queen Street ❶ 028 9032 5592 ❶ 09.00–16.00 Mon & Tues, 09.00–17.00 Wed, Fri & Sat, 09.00–19.30 Thur

Deanes Deli ££ ❺ Michelin-star chef Michael Deane's New York-style deli with olives, charcuterie boards, burgers, salads and soup for lunch and steaks and fish and chips in the evening. The adjacent store sells Deane's branded products. ⓐ 44 Bedford Street ❶ 028 9024 8800 ⓦ www.michaeldeane.co.uk ❶ 12.00–15.00, 17.00–21.00 Mon & Tues, 12.00–15.00, 17.00–22.00 Wed–Fri, 12.00–22.00 Sat

AFTER DARK

RESTAURANTS
The Red Panda £ ❻ Renowned Chinese restaurant in the Golden Mile. ⓐ 60 Great Victoria Street ❶ 028 9080 8700 ❶ 12.00–15.00, 17.00–23.30 Mon–Fri, 16.00–23.30 Sat, 13.30–22.30 Sun

Deanes ££ ❼ Sophisticated brasserie where you can treat yourself to dishes such as Portavogie fish and chips, roast monkfish or rack of lamb. ⓐ 36–40 Howard Street ❶ 028 9033 1134 ❶ 028 9056 0001 ⓦ www.michaeldeane.co.uk ❶ 12.00–15.00, 18.00–22.00 Mon–Sat

The Grill Room & Bar ££ ❽ Stop for a cocktail or two, and maybe a steak or some scampi, and hear the house band every Wed,

Thur and Sun. **ⓐ** Ten Square Hotel, 10 Donegall Square South **ⓣ** 028 9024 1001 **ⓦ** www.tensquare.co.uk **ⓛ** 07.30–01.00 Mon–Sat, 08.00–00.00 Sun; food served till 10pm

Hill Street Brasserie ££ ⑨ Cathedral Quarter restaurant serving modern Mediterranean dishes using fresh ingredients; one of the first to ban smoking. **ⓐ** 38 Hill Street **ⓣ** 028 9058 6868 **ⓦ** www.hillstbrasserie.com **ⓛ** 12.00–15.00 Mon–Sat, 17.00–23.00 Tues–Sat, 17.00–21.00 Sun

James Street South ££ ⑩ European cuisine in contemporary surroundings with set lunch and pre-theatre menus. **ⓐ** 21 James Street South **ⓣ** 028 9043 4310 **ⓦ** www.jamesstreetsouth.co.uk **ⓛ** 12.00–14.45 & 17.45–22.45 Mon–Sat, 17.30–21.00 Sun

Zen Restaurant £££ ⑪ Excellent Japanese restaurant serving sushi, sashimi and fusion food. **ⓐ** 55–59 Adelaide Street **ⓣ** 028 9023 2244 **ⓛ** 12.00–15.00 & 17.00–23.30 Mon–Fri, 18.00–01.00 Sat, 13.30–22.00 Sun

BARS & CLUBS

Café Vaudeville A former bank that was transformed into one of the city's glitziest bars. A couple of years after opening, it's as popular as ever, with its extravagant mix of high ceilings, chandeliers and gilt-frame pictures. Stop for coffee, tea, modern European food, beers and cocktails, or pre-book for the 'Bolly bar' upstairs. **ⓐ** 25–39 Arthur Street **ⓣ** 028 9043 9160 **ⓦ** www.cafevaudeville.com **ⓛ** 11.30–01.00 Mon–Sat

Crown Liquor Saloon A pint in this historic Belfast pub is a must. Sit in a snug or at the bar with a pint or lunch in the Crown Dining Rooms upstairs, which features local specialities like sausage and champ. ⓐ 46 Great Victoria Street ⓣ 028 9027 9901 ⓦ www.crownbar.com

Duke of York One of the oldest pubs in the city, in its heyday it was frequented by the literati, politicians and hacks who worked in the nearby newspaper industry. Sit in a snug and enjoy a few pints and traditional Irish food. ⓐ Commercial Court, off Donegall Street, Cathedral Quarter ⓣ 028 9024 1062 ⓛ 11.30–23.00 Mon, 11.30–01.00 Tues–Sun

The John Hewitt Traditional music every night except Weds; popular with local artists, writers and journalists. ⓐ 51 Donegall Street ⓣ 028 9023 3768 ⓦ www.thejohnhewitt.com ⓛ 11.30–01.00 Mon–Fri, 12.00–01.00 Sat, doesn't always open on Sun

The Kitchen Bar This famous old bar was once the haunt of visiting stars of the stage but was moved to make way for the new Victoria Square shopping centre. Now located in a former Victorian warehouse at its entrance, there's food, live music in the bar and sports on the plasma screens. ⓐ 36–40 Victoria Square ⓣ 028 9032 4901 ⓛ 12.00–23.00 Mon–Thur, 12.00–01.00 Fri & Sat, 12.00–21.00 Sun

Kremlin Now Belfast's veteran gay bar, Kremlin has recently had a makeover and hosts dance and indie, as well as camp cabaret shows. ⓐ 96 Donegall Street ⓣ 028 9031 6060

ⓦ www.kremlin-belfast.com ⓛ 21.00–02.30 Tues,
21.00–03.00 Thur–Sun

The Limelight/Spring & Airbrake/Katy Daly's Three venues in
one, Katy Daly's is a good place for cheap eats. The Limelight
is Belfast's best live music venue, closely followed by Spring
& Airbrake. They also host gay discos, DJ nights and stand-up
comedy. ⓐ 15–17 Ormeau Avenue ⓣ 028 9032 5968
ⓦ www.the-limelight.co.uk ⓛ Varies

Mynt Formerly Parliament, this was Belfast's first gay bar and
is still its biggest with a lounge bar and two club rooms with
more in the pipeline. You can eat international food here,
stop for a drink or stay for karaoke nights, game shows and
occasional live music. ⓐ 2–16 Dunbar Street ⓣ 028 9023 4520
ⓦ www.myntbelfast.com ⓛ 12.00–23.30 Mon & Tues,
12.00–00.30 Wed, 12.00–02.00 Thur, 12.00–05.00 Fri,
12.00–06.00 Sat, 12.00–03.00 Sun

Robinson's Bars Four venues under one roof, including the saloon
bar Fibber Magee's in the back with live traditional music, BT1
basement chill-out bar and Mezza(nine) club. ⓐ 38–42 Great
Victoria Street ⓣ 028 9024 7447 ⓦ www.robinsonsbar.co.uk
ⓛ 11.30–01.00 Mon–Sat, 12.30–00.00 Sun

White's Tavern Claims to be the oldest pub in Belfast, just off
High Street. Homemade food is served during the day and there
are live bands every Fri, Sat and Sun. ⓐ 2–4 Winecellar Entry
ⓣ 028 9024 3080 ⓦ www.whitestavern.co.uk ⓛ 11.30–23.00

North & West Belfast

The Falls and Shankill roads are among the most notorious in Belfast, a hotspot for nationalist and loyalist clashes during The Troubles, but these areas had been divided along religious lines way before the recent conflict. When migrants poured into Belfast during the Industrial Revolution they flocked to areas that were already either Catholic or Protestant, bringing their rivalries with them. The Shankill Road, which stands between West Belfast and North Belfast, was actually the sight of settlements dating back to the Stone Age, but its name derives from the Gaelic *Sean Cill*, meaning 'old church'. Today there's nothing Gaelic about the Shankill and despite the official end of the armed struggle, it remains run down, struggling to rebuild its community, displaying its identity through murals and flags. Tourists are attracted here to see the murals and the peace line that divides it from the Catholic Falls Road. A symbol of Republican West Belfast, the Falls Road was extremely deprived, maybe even more so in the 1960s, but today it is celebrating its Irishness with Irish names, Celtic script on signs and Irish cultural centres and sports. You should visit the murals in both areas to begin to understand the origins and impact of the conflict. In general most visitors prefer to eat, drink and stay in the city centre or South Belfast, but the locals are encouraging tourism by opening their own B&Bs. Overlooking West Belfast, the hills of Cave Hill Country Park are a must-see, with Belfast Castle, its Visitor Centre and trails to McArt's Fort providing an insight into the city's history. Nearby Belfast Zoo provides light relief for children.

SIGHTS & ATTRACTIONS

Belfast Castle

The original Belfast Castle was built by the Normans in the 12th century in what is now the city centre (Castle Street). Another castle followed on the same site, but this was burned down in the early 18th century, and it was the Marquis of Donegall who commissioned the current building on the slopes of Cave Hill. It was finished in 1870 and presented to the City of Belfast in 1934. It has been a popular location for weddings, dances and afternoon teas ever since. You can visit the castle but access depends on what events are taking place. There is also a shop and restaurant, as well as a Visitor Centre on the second floor

⬤ *Cave Hill Country Park overlooks the city*

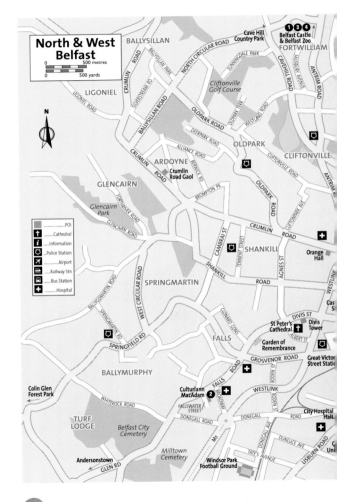

North & West Belfast

0 ___ 500 metres
0 ___ 500 yards

BALLYSILLAN

LIGONIEL

LIGONIEL ROAD

CRUMLIN ROAD

SILVERSTREAM RD

BALLYSILLAN PARK

BALLYSILLAN ROAD

NORTH CIRCULAR ROAD

CRUMLIN ROAD

Cave Hill Country Park

Belfast Castle & Belfast Zoo

FORTWILLIAM

CAVEHILL ROAD

ANTRIM ROAD

SALISBURY AVENUE

CUNNINGDALE PARK

Cliftonville Golf Course

OLDPARK ROAD

DEERPARK ROAD

ALLIANCE ROAD

ARDOYNE

Crumlin Road Gaol

OLDPARK TERR

OLDPARK

WESTLAND ROAD

BERWICK RD

CLIFTONVILLE

CLIFTONVILLE ROAD

GLENCAIRN

Glencairn Park

FORTWILLIAM ROAD

GLENCAIRN ROAD

CRUMLIN ROAD

BROMPTON PK

OLDPARK ROAD

CLIFTONVILLE AVE

ANTRIM

CAMBRAI ST

CRUMLIN ROAD

SHANKILL

TENNENT STREET

AGNES ST

Orange Hall

SPRINGMARTIN

SHANKILL

ROAD

WESTLINK

BALLYGOMARTIN ROAD

WEST CIRCULAR ROAD

SPRINGMARTIN RD

SPRINGFIELD RD

CONWAY CONS

FALLS

DIVIS ST

St Peter's Cathedral

Divis Tower

ALBERT ST

Cas S

SPRINGFIELD ROAD

Garden of Remembrance

Great Victor Street Statio

BALLYMURPHY

FALLS ROAD

BROADWAY

GROSVENOR ROAD

RODEN ST

JS ROSS ROAD

WESTLINK

City Hospital Halt

Colin Glen Forest Park

WHITEROCK ROAD

Culturlann MacAdam

FALLSWATER STREET

DONEGALL ROAD

DONEGALL

ROAD

DUNLUCE AVE

Ui

TURF LODGE

Belfast City Cemetery

M1

DONEGALL AVE

LISBURN ROAD

Andersonstown

GLEN RD

Milltown Cemetery

Windsor Park Football Ground

TATE'S AVENUE

Legend

POI
🛆 Cathedral
ℹ Information
⊙ Police Station
✈ Airport
🚆 Railway Stn
🚌 Bus Station
✚ Hospital

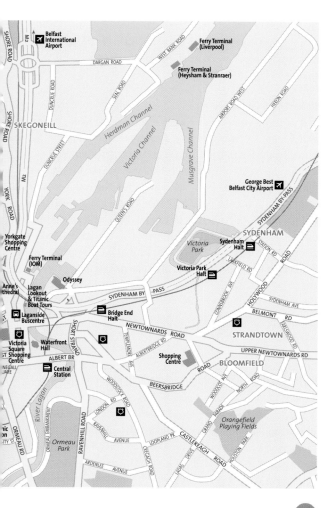

with exhibits on both the history of the castle and Cave Hill Country Park (see page 82). ⓐ Antrim Road ⓣ 028 9077 6925 ⓦ www.belfastcastle.co.uk ⓛ 09.00–22.00 Mon–Sat, 09.00–18.00 Sun ⓝ Bus: 1A-D

Belfast City Cemetery

Belfast City Cemetery is a mixed cemetery located in a nationalist area. Before it opened in 1869, a wall was built underground to symbolically divide the Catholic and Protestant areas. Look out for the graves of some famous Belfast residents, including the writer Robert Wilson Lynd, Viscount Pirrie (chairman of Harland and Wolff during the building of the Titanic), Sir Edward Harland (one of the founders of Harland and Wolff) and Denis Donaldson, former IRA member and Sinn Féin official, who was killed in 2006 after it was announced that he had been a spy for the British Government. Tours are available. ⓐ Falls Road ⓣ 028 9032 0202 ⓛ 08.00–18.00 Mon–Sat, 10.00–18.00 Sun Mar & Oct; 08.00–18.00 Mon, Wed, Fri & Sat, 08.00–20.00 Tues & Thur, 10.00–18.00 Sun Apr–Sept; 08.00–16.00 Mon–Sat, 10.00–16.00 Sun Nov–Feb ⓝ Bus: 10A-F

Belfast Zoo

Located in North Belfast near the Castle (see page 77), the zoo aims to help endangered species of animals from around the world. Divided into continental areas, you can see Rothschild's giraffe, gorilla and the white-crested turaco in Africa, leaf monkey, tiger and elephant in Asia, and the Andean bear, spider monkey and vincuña in South America, among others. You can also eat at The Ark Restaurant or The Mountain Teahouse.

ⓐ Antrim Road ⓣ 028 9077 6277 ⓦ www.belfastzoo.co.uk
ⓛ 10.00–17.00 Apr–Sept; 10.00–14.30 Oct–Mar ⓝ 10A-F, 2A.
Admission charge

Black Cab Tours NI

A good alternative to other official tours, the Black Cab Tours offer an insiders' view of the city. Belfast tours take in the Shankill and Falls Road murals, Milltown Cemetery, Stormont, Queen's University, City Hall and Belfast Castle. It is more expensive, but you can stop to take pictures or buy souvenirs and can ask

● *Black cab tours take in the famous murals*

questions as you go. You can also hire cabs to go on a Causeway Coast tour or devise your own itinerary. ① 07754 095736 ⓦ www.blackcabtoursni.com ⊙ By arrangement ⊗ Drivers will pick you up at your hotel if required

Cave Hill Country Park

Rising up 368 m (1,207 ft) behind the city, Cave Hill is one of the city's most celebrated landmarks and the location of Belfast Castle (see page 77). Since 1992 it has been a Country Park and wildlife refuge for a variety of animals and birds, as well as containing two nature reserves, Ballyhagan and Hazelwood. One of the most noticeable features of the park is Napoleon's Nose, an outcrop on the top of the hill, which can be seen from the city centre. Also known as McArt's Fort, It was here that the leaders of the 1798 rebellion took an oath to fight for Ireland's liberation from English rule. You can discover more about the history of the area at the Visitor Centre inside the Castle and also explore the park via way-marked paths. ⓐ Antrim Road ⊙ Dawn till dusk ⊗ Bus: 1A-F

Coiste Political Tours

Another way to see the city is to take a tour round republican and loyalist areas with the ex-prisoner community. Starting from Divis Tower at the Westlink end of the Falls Road, you get to hear some very different viewpoints on the conflict. The walking tours last around two hours, but booking is essential – you can even organise tours in Spanish, Basque, Irish or French. ⓐ Divis Tower, Falls Road ① 028 9020 0770 ⓦ www.coiste.ie ⊙ Walking tour: 11.00 Mon–Sat; 14.00 Sun ⊗ Walk or take collective black taxi from Castle Street car park. Admission charge

Crumlin Road Gaol Tour

This former prison was opened in the 19th century and finally closed in 1996. It held political prisoners throughout the 20th century and became notorious during The Troubles as a remand centre. Now in a state of repair, there is talk of turning it into a visitor centre or museum. Meantime, you can take a guided tour of the gaol and the tunnel that links it to the Court House, which is also awaiting redevelopment. Tours should be booked in advance. ⓐ Crumlin Road ☎ 028 9024 6609 ⏰ 10.00–16.45 Fri & Sat, 11.30–16.00 Sun, June–Sept Ⓝ Bus: 12

Divis Tower

Divis Tower might seem like any ordinary tower block, but from the 1970s the top two floors were occupied by the British army as a lookout point over Divis flats around the tower (which were demolished in the early 1980s), up the Falls Road and towards the city centre. The troops finally moved out in 2005, but the tower is still an iconic building in the history of The Troubles. ⓐ Divis Street Ⓝ Walk from city centre or take black taxi from Castle Street car park

Garden of Remembrance

Walking up the Falls Road, just before you arrive at the library and Sinn Féin bookshop on the right-hand side, you'll see a small garden on the left. This is one of many memorials to those who died in The Troubles. Being in the Falls Road, this is dedicated to republicans (including the hunger striker Bobby Sands), with the Irish tricolour flying above. ⓐ Falls Road Ⓝ Walk from city centre or take a black taxi from Castle Street car park

Milltown Cemetery

Located along the Falls Road, this is a Catholic cemetery where you'll find IRA and other republican memorials. A sea of Celtic crosses, the cemetery has a backdrop of the Belfast hills and views across the M1 motorway towards the city centre. Look out for the green field of unmarked paupers' graves, where victims of cholera, typhoid and flu were buried. ⓐ Falls Road ⓝ Bus: 10A-F. Walk from city centre or take black taxi from Castle Street car park

Orange Hall

As you cross the Westlink towards Crumlin Road, you will see an Orange Hall on the left-hand side. On the top is a statue of 'King Billy', William of Orange, who defeated King James I in the famous Battle of the Boyne in 1690. Today this is a renowned starting point for Orange Order marches. ⓐ Carlisle Circus ⓝ Bus: 1A, 1B, 1E

MILLTOWN: REFLECTING BELFAST'S TROUBLED PAST

In 1988, the loyalist paramilitary Michael Stone killed two mourners and a Provisional IRA member, and injured around 50 more people at a funeral at Milltown Cemetery for the Gibraltar Three (three IRA members killed by the SAS in Gibraltar). The cemetery also contains the graves of Bobby Sands and the other hunger strikers who died in 1981. Look at the plots more carefully and you'll notice that the republican plots are divided up into Official IRA, Provisional IRA, INLA and Real IRA.

🔺 *A sea of Celtic crosses: Milltown Cemetery*

Peace Line

This is a steel wall that divides the nationalist Falls Road area from the loyalist Shankill Road. The best way to see it is on the sightseeing bus tour. ⓐ West Belfast Ⓝ Bus: 10A-F

St Peter's Cathedral

Belfast's Roman Catholic cathedral was built in the 19th century to cope with the large numbers of workers who had come to work in the linen mills nearby. Its position made it a prominent landmark with five doorways, two porch entrances and a sculpture depicting the liberation of St Peter from prison over the main entrance, plus its iconic twin spires, which were added a few years later. ⓐ St Peter's Square, off Albert Street ⓣ 028 9032 7573 ⓕ 028 9032 5570 ⓦ www.stpeterscathedralbelfast.com ⓛ Mass: 10.00 Mon–Sat, 19.30 Tues & Thur, 09.00, 11.00, 19.00 Sun

West Belfast Murals

The political murals in West Belfast have become one of the city's most popular tourist attractions. You can get a quick overview on a bus tour but to get a closer look you either need to take a private black cab tour (see page 81) or go on foot. There are some interesting murals in East Belfast too but they are not as accessible as those along the nationalist Falls Road and the loyalist Shankill Road. You'll see murals on the side of virtually every corner building along the streets. In the Falls Road these range from murals showing sympathy for other nationalist and liberation movements, such as those in Palestine and Catalonia and images depicting the 1916 Easter Rising, hunger strikers and other 'fallen' IRA comrades. Along the Shankill Road you can see images of the Derry Apprentice Boys slamming the gates of the city in 1688 and the Battle of the Boyne in 1690, as well as murals supporting loyalist paramilitary groups such as the Ulster Volunteer Force (UVF) and Ulster Defence Association (UDA). ⓐ Falls and Shankill Roads ◎ Sightseeing bus tour, black taxi tour or on foot

CULTURE

Cultúrlann MacAdam

The centre of the Falls Road Gaeltacht (Irish-speaking) community, it runs Irish language courses, has a bookshop and tourist point (with help on accommodation), and hosts art, music, drama and literature events. Hear some live traditional Irish music in the café/restaurant every week – they welcome passing musicians too! Buy an Irish language course in the shop, hear locals chatting in Irish in the café or stay for one of the other events. ⓐ 216 Falls Road ❶ 028 9096 4180 ⓦ www.culturlann.com ❶ 09.00–21.00 Mon–Fri, 09.00–18.00 Sat & Sun ◎ Any bus from Queen Street in the city centre

RETAIL THERAPY

At Cultúrlann, there's a selection of Irish language and literature books as well as cards and photographs. In Andersonstown there's a large O'Neills International Sportswear shop selling Gaelic football strip, hurley sticks and balls, Ireland rugby tops and Celtic football tops.

TAKING A BREAK

The Ark Café £ ❶ Located in Belfast Zoo, this is a good option for the family with hot and cold food and veggie options. ⓐ Belfast Zoo ⓣ 028 9077 6925 ⓦ www.belfastzoo.co.uk ⓛ 10.30–17.30 Apr–Sept, 10.30–15.30 Oct–Mar

Cultúrlann Café £ ❷ You can stop here for a late lunch, afternoon refreshments or dinner at a reasonable price, while listening to locals chatting in Irish (see page 87). The menu includes fish and chips, lasagne, burgers, wraps and pizzas. ⓐ 216 Falls Road ⓣ 028 9096 4180 ⓦ www.culturlann.com ⓛ 09.00–21.00 Mon–Fri, 09.00–18.00 Sat & Sun

The Mountain Teahouse £ ❸ Stop for a coffee, cake and biscuits or other snacks during a visit to Belfast Zoo. ⓐ Belfast Zoo, Antrim Road ⓣ 028 9077 6925 ⓦ www.belfastzoo.co.uk ⓛ 10.30–17.00 Apr–Sept

AFTER DARK

RESTAURANTS
Cellar Restaurant ££ ❹ This is Belfast Castle's restaurant and serves quality home-grown food in a beautiful historic location. ⓐ Belfast Castle, off Antrim Road ⓣ 028 9077 6925 ⓦ www.belfastcastle.co.uk ⓛ 11.00–17.00 (snacks/light refreshments), 12.30–15.00 (lunch) Mon–Sat, 17.00–18.30 (early evening meal), 19.00–21.00 (dinner) Tues–Sat

PUBS

The Beehive A lively local pub with pub grub from fish and chips to curry, plus folk sessions on a Sunday. ⓐ 193 Falls Road ⓣ 028 9032 8439 ⓛ 11.30–23.00 Mon–Sat, 12.00–22.30 Sun

McEnaney's Located opposite Milltown Cemetery, stop at this traditional pub for a pint or two after a long walk from the city centre and if you're lucky you might hear some live traditional music. ⓐ Glen Road, Andersonstown ⓣ 028 9061 3951 ⓛ 11.30–00.00 Mon–Sat, 12.00–00.00 Sun

P & F Gil Martin Traditional Victorian pub with original décor and tiled floor, this is what was considered a 'man's pub', where men would bring their wives at weekends only. They can now come any night of the week (who said Emily Davison died in vain?), but they still have to drink separately upstairs! ⓐ Lower Springfield Road ⓛ 11.30–23.00 Mon–Sat, 12.00–22.30 Sun

South & East Belfast

South and East Belfast are adjacent but contrasting areas of Belfast. As the location of Queen's University, the South is considered to be the intellectual centre, but its large student population also gives it a bohemian feel. Cheap student terraced accommodation backs on to leafy avenues of expensive houses; boutique hotels and designer clothes shops along the Lisburn Road lead into wild nights in Bradbury Place and Botanic Avenue. You can walk to Botanic easily from the city centre and even down to Queen's University if you have the feet for it. Beyond that and you'll have to think about taking a bus. Make time to see East Belfast, primarily a residential area but also the location of some key attractions and the gateway to North Down. Take a tour round the Titanic Quarter, the target of a huge makeover that will transform the area and bring work, play, arts, cafés and hotels.

SIGHTS & ATTRACTIONS

Belfast Titanic Trail

This interactive trail is a self-guided tour using a hand-held media player. It takes you on a multi-media tour of the key city sights associated with the RMS Titanic, from City Hall to Queen's Island. It is available for hire from the Belfast Welcome Centre. ⓐ Belfast Welcome Centre, 47 Donegall Place ⓣ 028 9024 6609 ⓦ www.gotobelfast.com ⓛ 09.00–17.00 Mon–Sat Oct–May; 09.00–19.00 Mon–Sat, 12.00–17.00 Sun June–Sept ⓝ Bus: Donegall Square. Admission charge

Botanic Gardens Park

Highlights of the park are the restored Victorian Palm House, with a valuable collection of tropical and temperate palms, and Tropical Ravine, with a humid jungle glen and a fish pond filled with giant water lilies. Today it is popular with both locals and visitors for walking, relaxing and taking in the sights and sounds, including occasional events from pop and classical concerts to the annual Garden Gourmet in September.

ⓐ Stranmillis Road/Botanic Avenue ① 028 9032 0202 ① Dawn till dusk Ⓝ Bus: 8 to Queens University or 7 to College Park

Lagan Valley Regional Park

This park was established in 1967 and extends more than 10 miles from Stranmillis in South Belfast to Lisburn's Union Locks.

❏ *The Palm House at Botanic Gardens*

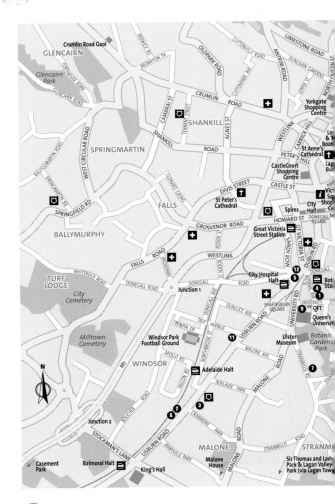

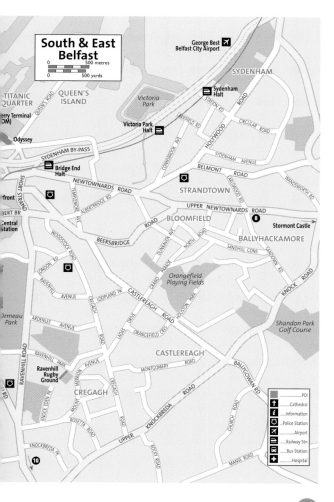

The reach of the park means it is a mosaic of countryside, urban parks, heritage sites, nature reserves and riverside trails. ⓐ Lockview Road to Lisburn Union Locks ☏ 028 9049 1922 ⓦ www.laganvalley.co.uk ⏱ 24 hours Ⓑ Bus: 8B-C, 8A

Malone House

Malone House is an elegant late Georgian manor located in the South Belfast parkland known as the Barnett Demesne, itself part of the Lagan Valley Regional Park. You can walk through woodland, meadows and marsh. Look out for rabbits, foxes, mink, otters, bats and long-eared owls. ⓐ Barnett Demesne, Malone Road ☏ 028 9068 1246 ⓦ www.malonehouse.co.uk ⏱ Park: 24 hours, Malone House: 09.00–17.00 Mon–Sat, 12.00–17.00 Sun Ⓑ Bus: 9A-C

Odyssey

A Landmark Millennium Project for Northern Ireland, the Odyssey complex is divided into three main parts:

W5 (ⓦ www.w5online.co.uk) is an interactive discovery centre with four dynamic exhibition areas, Start, Go, See and Do, plus changing temporary exhibitions. Here kids (and adults) make a voyage of discovery. You can find out what it's like to be a car mechanic, explore your senses with the sounds and feel of nature in a woodland area, beat the lie detector and bring robots to life.

Odyssey Arena (ⓦ www.odysseyarena.com) is home to the Belfast Giants ice hockey team and also hosts touring shows, exhibitions and concerts.

Odyssey Pavilion (ⓦ www.odysseypavilion.com) where you'll find an IMAX cinema, ten-pin bowling, bars, restaurants and a nightclub, plus a large car park. ⓐ Queen's Quay ☏ 028 9045 1055

028 9045 1052 ⓦ www.theodyssey.co.uk ⓛ Various ⓝ Bus: Laganside or shuttle bus during major events from various city centre pick-up points. Admission charge

Ormeau Park

Once part of the demesne of the Donegall family, the estate was sold to the Belfast Corporation in the late 19th century, becoming the first public park in Belfast. It remains one of the largest in the city with woodland, wildlife and nature trails, and hosts various events throughout the year. ⓐ Ormeau Road ⓕ 028 9032 0202 ⓛ Dawn till dusk ⓝ Bus: 7A, 7D

Queen's University

Founded by Queen Victoria, Queen's University opened in 1840 in the magnificent Lanyon Building, still the most recognisable part of the university. Since then the university estate has grown to include more than 300 buildings. There is a visitor centre inside the Lanyon

Queen's University, built in prosperous Victorian times

Building, with a gift shop and exhibitions. ⓐ University Road
ⓣ 028 9097 5252 ⓦ www.qub.ac.uk ⓛ Welcome Centre: 10.00–16.00
Mon–Sat, 10.00–13.00 Sun (May–Sept Sat & Sun only) ⓝ Bus: 8A–C

Stormont Castle
The home of the Northern Ireland Executive, this neoclassical
building is located at the end of Prince of Wales Avenue. George
Best's funeral was held here in 2005. Unfortunately visitors can't
go inside but can walk along the avenue and in the grounds.
ⓐ Upper Newtownards Road ⓦ www.niassembly. gov.uk
ⓝ Bus: 23 to Stormont Massey Avenue Gates

Titanic Boat Tours
This water tour is a great way to learn all about the Titanic.
You'll see the offices where the ship was designed, the dry
dock where it was worked on and the slipways where it first
took to water. ⓐ No 2 jetty, Donegall Quay ⓣ 07718 910 423
ⓦ www.laganboatcompany.com ⓛ 12.30, 14.00, 15.30 mid-Feb–
mid-Dec (extra sailing at 11.00 Sat & Sun, June–Sept) ⓝ Bus:
Laganside Buscentre ❶ Book in advance. Admission charge

Titanic Quarter
Once the centre of Belfast's great shipbuilding industry, today
the former shipyards on Queen's Island are referred to as the
Titanic Quarter, as the RMS Titanic was designed and built here
by the company Harland and Wolff which was set up in the
1860s. Today the company is a leader in ship repair, design and
structural engineering, and the shipyards are once again seeing
some activity with new plans for development. Harland and

BUILDING THE TITANIC

By the time Edward Harland died in 1895, Harland and Wolff had become the world's greatest shipbuilders. Designed by Alexander Carlisle and then Thomas Andrews, the floating palace that was the Titanic was launched on 31 May 1911 in front of thousands of onlookers. It was taken to Southampton and set off on its maiden voyage from there on 10 April 1912. Four days later, having travelled 1,500 miles, the ship struck an iceberg and was fatally damaged. Of the 2,228 passengers and crew, only 705 survived.

Wolff's two yellow cranes known as Samson and Goliath stand as a monument to the great shipbuilding era, but around them a new era has begun. As part of the development over the next decade, apartments, hotels, offices, marinas and cultural spaces are already being built onsite. Visitors can visit Thompson Dock and Pump House where RMS Titanic had its final fit-out. Take the Belfast Citysightseeing tour bus (see page 65) and hop off here to visit the Dry Dock and HMS Caroline. ⓐ Queen's Island ⓦ www.titanicquarter.com ⓝ Bus: Laganside Buscentre or Belfast Citysightseeing tour bus

CULTURE

Crescent Arts Centre

Housed in a former girls' school, this arts centre hosts workshops, education/outreach classes, exhibitions and events from drama,

dance and movement to music. ⓐ 2–4 University Road
ⓣ 028 9024 2338 ⓦ www.crescentarts. org ⓛ 10.00–22.00 variable
Mon–Fri, 10.00–19.00 variable Sat Ⓝ Bus: 9A-C. Admission charge

King's Hall

This large venue hosts exhibitions, conferences and events from
home, dog and bike shows to concerts and boxing matches.
ⓐ Lisburn Road, Balmoral ⓣ 028 9066 5225 ⓦ www.kingshall.co.uk
ⓛ Performance times vary – check website for details Ⓝ Train:
Balmoral Halt; Bus: 9B/9A to Lisburn Road. Admission charge

The Naughton Gallery at Queen's

Located inside Queen's University, this gallery exhibits works from
the university's own collection as well as touring exhibitions and
shows by local and international artists. It's only been in business
since 2001, but its dynamism and verve has already won it a
reputation as one of the leading academic-institution *vitrines* in
Europe; and quite right, too – no stuffy, conservative gallery, this,
the Naughton encourages experimental artists and fosters the
development of promising newcomers. It also regularly stages
fascinating lectures by visiting glitter-arty types. ⓐ Lanyon Building,
Queen's University ⓣ 028 9097 3580 ⓦ www.naughtongallery.org
ⓛ 11.00–16.00 Mon–Sat Ⓝ Bus: 8A-C

Queen's Film Theatre

Ireland's longest-established cultural cinema, the QFT, screens
both classics and contemporary films. ⓐ 20 University Square
ⓣ 028 9097 1097 ⓦ www. queensfilmtheatre.com ⓛ Screening
times vary – check website for details Ⓝ Bus: 8A-C. Admission charge

Ulster Museum

With 8,000 sq m (5 sq miles) of galleries, you'll need two or three hours to get round this museum, but the investment of time – and maybe even energy – will be well worth it. Highlights of the permanent collection include Palaeolithic bones and Neolithic ceramics, medieval jewellery and remains of Armada wrecks, Old Masters and Irish paintings from the 17th century to the present. Adding to the cornucopia are sculpture, furniture, fashion, photos and militaria. ⓐ Botanic Gardens, Stranmillis Road ⓣ 028 9038 3000 ⓦ www.ulstermuseum.org.uk
ⓛ 10.00–17.00 Mon–Fri, 13.00–17.00 Sat, 14.00–17.00 Sun
ⓣ Train: Botanic; Bus: 8A/8B from Donegall Square East

TAKING A BREAK

Café Vincent £ ❶ Continental-style café serving sandwich and soup lunches as well as an international menu at dinner. ⓐ 78–80 Botanic Avenue ⓣ 028 9024 2020 ⓛ 10.30–22.00

Cargoes £ ❷ Serves coffee and deli foods from feta and olives to pasta and soup. ⓐ 613 Lisburn Road ⓣ 028 9066 5451

Clements £ ❸ One of a small chain of coffee bars with seven outlets in Belfast. They pride themselves on their quality coffee and cakes. ⓐ 342 Lisburn Road ⓣ 028 9033 1827 ⓛ 08.00–00.00 Mon–Thur, 08.00–23.00 Fri, 09.00–23.00 Sat, 10.00–23.00 Sun

Maggie May's Belfast Café £ ❹ This is the place to come for hangover food or if you're just after a good Ulster fry for

breakfast. ⓐ 50 Botanic Avenue ⓣ 028 9032 2662
ⓛ 08.00–22.30 Mon–Sat, 10.00–22.30 Sun

Revelations Internet Café £ ❺ Grab a frappucino, ice cream
milkshake or herbal tea and check your email at the same time.
ⓐ 27 Shaftesbury Square ⓣ 028 9032 0337 ⓦ www.revelations.co.uk
ⓛ 08.00–22.00 Mon–Fri, 10.00–18.00 Sat, 11.00–19.00 Sun

Ruby Tuesday's £ ❻ Mediterranean-style café with everything
from an Ulster fry to pasta and salads. ⓐ 629A Lisburn Road
ⓣ 028 9059 3401 ⓛ 08.15–22.00 Mon–Sat

AFTER DARK

RESTAURANTS
The Blue Print Pizza Company £ ❼ Easy lunch or dinner stop in
the heart of the university district with pizzas, pasta and salads.
ⓐ 92 Stranmillis Road ⓣ 028 9066 3101 ⓦ www.blueprintpizza.com
ⓛ 11.00–23.00 Mon–Sat, 13.00–23.00 Sun

Aldens Restaurant ££ ❽ Modern restaurant with a varied menu
which attracts local celebrities and politicians. ⓐ 229 Upper
Newtonards Road ⓣ 028 9065 0079 ⓦ www.aldensrestaurant.com
ⓛ 12.00–14.30 Mon–Fri; 18.00–22.00 Mon–Thur; 18.00–23.00
Fri & Sat

Beatrice Kennedy ££ ❾ One of Belfast's finest restaurants,
there's an intimate but relaxed atmosphere here and a modern
menu that features the likes of Portavogie crab meat, seared

local scallops and rare breed pork loin. ⓐ 44 University Road
ⓣ 028 9020 2290 ⓦ www. beatricekennedy.co.uk ⓛ 17.00–22.15
Tues–Sat, 12.30–14.30 & 17.00–20.15 Sun

Four Winds ££ ❿ Venue divided into three parts: the top-
floor Ink Restaurant with panoramic city views; slick Blue
Glass Wine Bar; and the latest addition, Lounge, a new-age bar.
ⓐ 111 Newton Park ⓣ 028 9070 7970 ⓦ www.thefourwinds.co.uk
ⓛ Variable

Shu Restaurant ££ ⓫ Brasserie-style ground-floor restaurant,
basement cocktail and tapas bar with top Belfast DJs on
the decks every Wednesday. The head chef is winner of the
All-Ireland award. ⓐ 253 Lisburn Road ⓣ 028 9038 1655
ⓦ www.shu-restaurant.com ⓛ 12.00–14.30 & 18.00–22.00
Mon–Sat

Cayenne £££ ⓬ Award-winning restaurant owned by celebrity
chefs Paul and Jeanne Rankin serving modern Irish cuisine with
an international flavour. ⓐ 7 Ascot House, Shaftesbury Square
ⓣ 028 9033 1532 ⓦ www.rankingroup.co.uk ⓛ 12.00–14.15 Tues–Fri,
17.00–22.15 Sun–Thur, 17.00–23.15 Fri, 18.00–23.15 Sat

CLUBS & PUBS

The Botanic Inn Another favourite pub with three different
bars offering live sports, pub grub, live music and the
odd pub quiz. ⓐ 23–27 Malone Road ⓣ 028 9050 9740
ⓦ www.thebotanicinn.com ⓛ 11.30–01.00 Mon–Sat,
12.00–00.00 Sun

Empire Music Hall Legendary establishment with a basement pub-style bar and old theatre-style upper venue with a stage featuring salsa classes, live music and comedy. ⓐ 42 Botanic Avenue ⓣ 028 9024 9276 ⓦ www.thebelfastempire.com ⓛ 11.00–01.00 Mon–Sat, 11.00–00.00 Sun

Lavery's Bar and Gin Palace Golden Mile venue notorious for the interesting characters that hang out here. A good raucous night out with food, music, pool hall, DJs and live music. ⓐ Bradbury Place, off Shaftesbury Square ⓣ 028 9087 1106 ⓦ www.laverysbelfast.com ⓛ 12.00–late

Madison's Boutique hotel with a café-bar upstairs serving food, beer and cocktails all day, with live music and club nights on Mondays and Fridays in The Avenue downstairs. ⓐ 59–63 Botanic Avenue ⓣ 028 9050 9800 ⓦ www.madisonshotel.com ⓛ 07.00–01.00

▶ *Giant's Causeway: a must-see*

Bangor & County Down

County Down is within easy reach of Belfast city centre. A few miles past George Best City Airport and the horizon widens as you head towards Holywood and Bangor overlooking Belfast Lough, an easy reach for day trips to the beach, country parks and the award-winning Ulster Folk & Transport Museum. South of here is Strangford Lough, with the Ards Peninsular on its east side. A trip to Downpatrick, one of the most important Christian sites in the country and the resting place of Ireland's patron Saint Patrick, is also possible in a day. With a few extra days you could spend some time in the seaside resort of Newcastle, tasting some of the freshest seafood, climbing the peaks of the Mourne Mountains and exploring the Norman castle at Dundrum.

GETTING THERE

There are various routes out of Belfast to County Down by car. For North Down, head out on the A2 past George Best City Airport to Holywood and Bangor or the A20 to Newtownards, which continues along the eastern banks of Strangford Lough to Portaferry. Alternatively you can take the A21/A22 down the west side towards Downpatrick. For Dundrum, Newcastle and the Mourne Mountains go south out of the city along the A24, and for Hillsborough take the M1 and A1.

Trains leave Central Station to Holywood and Bangor. Buses for Newtownards and Portaferry leave from Laganside Buscentre, but for Hillsborough, Downpatrick and Newcastle you'll need to go to Europa Buscentre.

SIGHTS & ATTRACTIONS

Ballyholme Beach

Ballyholme is a small coastal village between Bangor and Groomsport (see page 108), best known for its mile-long sandy beach. It's a favourite with families due to its gentle surf and the nearby nature reserve at Ballymacormick Point. ❷ Ballyholme Ⓝ Bus: BE4 (from Bangor)

Bangor

Bangor is a large seaside town with plenty of hotels, restaurants and entertainment, and is popular with tourists during the summer months. Bangor Marina is one of the largest in Northern Ireland. Look out for the rare colony of guillemots nesting in the harbour wall – they're also known as 'Bangor penguins'. Other highlights include: Bangor Abbey, a mixture of 15th–19th-century architecture; Bangor Castle, an Elizabethan-Jacobean-style mansion that is now actually the Town Hall; and the Tower House on Bangor seafront, which was built in 1637 as the Custom House and today is home to the tourist information centre. ❷ Bangor, Down ❶ Bangor Tourist Information 028 9127 0069 Ⓝ Train: Bangor

Downpatrick

The county town of County Down, Downpatrick, is associated with St Patrick, who is buried in the cemetery of **Down Cathedral**, along with St Columba and St Bridget. St Patrick is said to have brought Christianity to Ireland and for this reason this site is considered one of the holiest Christian sites in Ireland, dating from way before the construction of the 19th-century Gothic

Belfast region

0	20km
0	10 miles

shmills
Vhitepark Bay
Carrick-a-Rede
Rope Bridge
Rathlin Island
Ballintoy
Ballycastle Bay
Giant's Causeway
Iuce
tle
Armoy
Ballycastle
Ballymoney
Antrim
Hills
Cushendun
Cushendall
Clogh
Glencariff
Forest Park
Glens of
Antrim
Carnlough
M2
Glenarm
The Maidens
SCOTLAND
Ilymena
Moorfields
A36
Ballygalley Head
Larne
Stranraer
M22
Ballyclare
A8
Portmuck
The Gobbins
Antrim
M2
Carrickfergus
Belfast
International
Holywood
Carrickfergus Castle
Newtownabbey
Bangor
Ballyholme Beach
ugh
eagh
BELFAST
George Best
Belfast City
Groomsport
Ulster Folk
Museum
Scrabo Hill
Country Park
Newtownards
Lisburn
Comber
Ards
Peninsula
M1
A3
Sprucefield
Strangford
Lough
Lurgan
Hillsborough
ortadown
Portavogie
Bann
Banbridge
Castle Ward
Portaferry
Inch Abbey
Exploris
Poyntz Pass
Aso
Downpatrick
Castlewellan
A25
Dundrum
ewry
Tollymore
Forest Park
Mourne
Mountains
852
Slieve
Donard
Dundrum
Castle
Newcastle
Dundrum
Bay
Ardglass
ostrevor
Glasdrumman

Belfast region

○	City
○	Large Town
○	Small Town
■	POI
▬	Motorway
▬	Main Road
▬	Minor Road
✈	Airport

cathedral that stands here today. ⓐ English Street ⓣ 028 4461 4922
ⓦ www.downcathedral.org ⓛ 09.30–16.30 Mon–Sat,
14.00–17.00 Sun

Across the car park from the St Patrick Centre (see box)
you'll see **Downpatrick Railway**, a historic steam railway that
will take you to Inch Abbey. ⓐ Market Street ⓣ 028 4461 5779
ⓦ www.downrail.co.uk ⓛ 13.40–17.00 specific days (see website
or call for information). Admission charge.

Next to the cathedral, **Down County Museum** is located
on the site of a former gaol and military barracks where
United Irishman Thomas Russell was hanged in 1803. Today it
houses a vast collection of archaeological and historic exhibits
from the county. ⓐ The Mall, English Street ⓣ 028 4461 5218
ⓦ www.downcountymuseum.com ⓛ 10.00–17.00 Mon–Fri,
13.00–17.00 Sat & Sun

Dundrum Castle

Originally built by John de Courcy in the 12th century, Dundrum
is one of the finest Norman castles in Northern Ireland, with
panoramic views of Dundrum Bay, the Mourne Mountains and
the surrounding countryside. You can climb the round keep.
ⓐ Dundrum Village ⓣ 028 9181 1491 ⓦ www.ehsni.gov.uk
ⓛ 09.00–18.00 Tues–Sat, 13.00–18.00 Sun, Apr–Sept;
10.00–18.00 Sat, Oct–Mar ⓝ Bus: Dundrum

Groomsport

A charming seaside village two miles east of Bangor, with a
harbour, sandy beach and plenty of pubs and restaurants. Once
a fishing village, today it is a popular stop-off for day trippers

and sailing enthusiasts. Look out for the whitewashed Cockle Row Cottages, home to fishermen at the beginning of the 20th century. ⓐ Groomsport Ⓝ Bus: 3 (from Bangor)

Hillsborough

Several times winner of the most beautiful village in Northern Ireland prize, Hillsborough doesn't disappoint, with pretty terraced cottages with hanging baskets, boutiques, cafés and pubs selling good grub. Behind the main square you'll find **Hillsborough Castle** (ⓐ The Square ⓣ 028 9268 3368), official residence of the Secretary of State for Northern Ireland.

IRELAND'S PATRON SAINT

Kidnapped from his home in Britain as a teenager, St Patrick spent six years as a slave in County Antrim, before escaping and becoming a missionary, returning to Ireland to convert the Irish to Christianity. According to legend, he taught the Irish people the concept of the trinity using the three-leaved shamrock. At the bottom of Down Hill, where the cathedral stands, is the modern **St Patrick Centre**, where you can learn about the saint's history, browse the souvenirs in the shop and have a cup of tea in the café. ⓐ 53A Lower Market Street ⓣ 028 4461 9000 Ⓦ www.saintpatrickcentre.com Ⓛ 10.00–17.00 Mon–Sat Oct–Mar; 09.30–17.30 Mon–Sat, 13.00–17.30 Sun Apr, May & Sept; 09.30–18.00 Mon–Sat, 10.00–18.00 Sun June–Aug. Admission charge

Unfortunately it's only open a few days a year. Head through the square and downhill and follow signs to Hillsborough Forest Park on the left-hand side. ⓐ Tourist Information, The Square, Hillsborough ⓣ 028 9268 9717 ⓝ Bus: Hillsborough

Mourne Mountains

You don't have to be a hard-core hiker to appreciate the Mournes: this is, quite simply, one of the most stunning spots in Northern Ireland. For a lovely jaunt, drive to Tollymore Forest Park with its gentle woodland strolls or bravely tackle Slieve Donard, Northern Ireland's highest peak. There are plenty of other outdoor activities here from canoeing to orienteering (see page 36). ⓐ Newcastle ⓦ www.mournemountains.com ⓝ Bus: Newcastle

⬤ Cocklerow Cottage at Groomsport

Newcastle

A popular seaside resort at the foot of the mountains, Newcastle has a sweeping bay looking out to the Irish Sea. It's a good base for exploring the Mourne Mountains, and is home to the Royal County Down golf course. ⊗ Bus: Newcastle

Strangford Lough

Strangford Lough is separated from the Irish Sea by the Ards Peninsula, a strip of land which extends south from Bangor to Portaferry. You can spend more than a day walking along nature trails and visiting all the attractions round the water. **Scrabo Hill Country Park**, northwest of the lough, is dominated by Scrabo Hill and the tower upon it, and there's a picnic site with great views over the lough (ⓐ off the A22/A21 ⓣ Tower 028 9181 1491 ⓛ 10.30–18.00 Sat–Thur).

At the southern tip of the lough, make a detour to see **Inch Abbey**, the ruins of a Cistercian abbey founded by John de Courcy in the 12th century. You can take the steam train from nearby Downpatrick (see page 105) through scenic countryside (ⓐ off the Downpatrick-Belfast road ⓛ open access all year). Heading east along the A25, you'll come to **Castle Ward**, and an 18th-century country mansion set in beautiful parkland, famous for its opera performances in the summer (ⓐ Strangford ⓣ 028 4488 1204 ⓛ Guided tours of the house: 13.00–18.00 public holidays, school holidays and weekends Mar–Sept; grounds: 10.00–20.00 May–Sept, 10.00–16.00 Oct–Apr ⊗ Bus: 16E from Downpatrick to Strangford).

From Strangford there's a ferry to and from Portaferry. Here the most popular attraction is **Exploris**, an aquarium with species

native to the shores of Northern Ireland, including bass, edible sea urchin, octopus and peacock worm. ⓐ The Rope Walk, Castle Street, Portaferry ⓣ 028 4272 8062 ⓦ www.exploris.org.uk ⓛ 10.00–18.00 Mon–Fri, 11.00–18.00 Sat, 12.00–18.00 Sun Apr–Aug; 10.00–17.00 Mon–Fri, 11.00–17.00 Sat, 13.00–17.00 Sun Sept–Mar. Admission charge

CULTURE

Ulster Folk & Transport Museum

One of the most popular attractions in Northern Ireland, this museum is set in over 170 acres of countryside. The Folk Museum comprises buildings from all over the province transported here, rebuilt and restored to give an authentic view of life in early 20th-century Ulster. In each cottage, mill and shop you'll meet 'residents' in period costume spinning at the wheel, cooking soda wheaten over the fire or serving behind the counter. The Transport Museum has a comprehensive display from horse-drawn carts to Irish-built motor cars, locomotives and the history of ship and aircraft building. You'll need a full day to get round the whole lot so bring a picnic, snack in the tea rooms or head to Cultra Manor for the Sunday carvery. ⓐ 153 Bangor Road, Cultra, Holywood ⓣ 028 9042 8428 ⓦ www.uftm.org.uk ⓔ uftm.info@magni.org.uk ⓛ 10.00–17.00 Mon–Fri, 10.00–18.00 Sat, 11.00–18.00 Sun Mar–June; 10.00–18.00 Mon–Sat, 11.00–18.00 Sun July–Sept; 10.00–16.00 Mon–Fri, 10.00–17.00 Sat, 11.00–17.00 Sun Oct–Feb ⓝ Bus: Museum entrance; Train: Cultra Halt. Admission charge

TAKING A BREAK

RESTAURANTS

Mario's Restaurant ££ As Italian restaurants go, this is just about as authentic as you can get and has great views over Dundrum Bay. Chef and owner Mario sources his fresh produce locally and

🔺 *Bangor Marina*

his staff have been with him for years – you'll definitely get a warm welcome here. ⓐ 65 South Promenade, Newcastle ⓣ 028 4372 3912 ⓛ 18.00–21.30 Wed–Sat, 12.30–14.30, 17.00–21.00 Sun

Mourne Seafood Bar ££ Some of the freshest seafood and fish dishes on the coast here. They even have their own mussel and oyster beds in Carlingford Lough and sell fresh fish to take home. During the week there's a two-course set price lunch. ⓐ 77 Main Street, Dundrum ⓣ 028 4375 1377 ⓦ www.mourneseafood.com ⓛ 12.00–21.00 Mon–Fri, closes Mon & Tues off-season

Restaurant 1614 ££ Located in Ireland's oldest coaching inn, this restaurant serves a combination of classical and modern cuisine. Also offers a set price bistro menu for two. ⓐ The Old Inn, Main Street, Crawfordsburn ⓣ 028 9185 3255 ⓦ www. theoldinn.com ⓛ 19.00–21.30 Mon–Sat, 12.30–14.30 Sun

Mitre Restaurant £££ Considered to be one of the best restaurants in Northern Ireland, with a fine dining set menu. ⓐ Culloden Hotel, Bangor Road, Holywood ⓣ 028 9042 1066 ⓦ www.hastingshotels.com ⓛ 19.00–21.30 Mon–Fri, 12.30–14.30, 19.00–21.00 Sun

ACCOMMODATION

HOTELS AND GUEST HOUSES
Tara Guest House £ Traditional town house with spacious rooms

and views of Bangor Marina. ⓐ 51 Princetown Road, Bangor
ⓣ 028 9145 8820 ⓦ www.taraguesthouse.co.uk

The Royal Hotel ££ Family-run hotel on Bangor seafront
with café, bar and restaurant. ⓐ 26–28 Quay Street, Bangor
ⓣ 028 9127 1866 ⓦ www.royalhotelbangor.com

The Old Inn £££ Located in Ireland's oldest coaching inn, famous
guests are said to include the highwayman Dick Turpin and
former US President George Bush (senior). Stay in cosy rooms
with four-poster beds. ⓐ Main Street, Crawfordsburn
ⓣ 028 9185 3255 ⓦ www.theoldinn.com

Slieve Donard £££ Impressive Victorian hotel and Newcastle's
finest with views of the Mourne Mountains and the Irish Sea
plus a luxury spa, restaurant with fine Irish cuisine and hotel
bar with live entertainment. ⓐ Downs Road, Newcastle
ⓣ 028 4372 1066 ⓦ www.hastingshotels.com

CAMPING AND HOSTELS

Newcastle Hostel £ Located right on the seafront near pubs
and restaurants. ⓐ 30 Downs Road ⓣ 028 4372 2133

Windsor Caravan Park £ One of many caravan parks along the
Dundrum Road, this one permits touring caravans and has hire
facilities. ⓐ A2 from Newcastle to Dundrum ⓣ 028 4372 3367

Antrim Coast

The Antrim Coast is one of the most beautiful parts of Northern Ireland. A stunning coastline of lush forest glens, sweeping bays, and turquoise seas during the summer, in the winter it is wild and romantic. Steeped in myth and legend with a history of settlement dating way back to the Neolithic era, there are many natural and man-made sights, including Giant's Causeway, Bushmills Distillery, Dunluce Castle, Carrick-a-Rede Rope Bridge, Rathlin Island and the spectacular drive along the coast, as well as picture-box villages such as Cushendun and Ballintoy and seaside towns at Ballycastle and Portrush.

GETTING THERE

Hiring a car gives you the freedom to explore the Antrim Coast at your leisure. Drive north out of Belfast along the M2, then take the M5 towards Carrickfergus (about 20 minutes from the city centre). From there take the A2 coast road. Ballintoy, Carrick-a-Rede, Giant's Causeway, and Bushmills are all within two hours' drive, with Portrush a further 15 minutes away. Ulsterbus run the Antrim Coaster from Laganside Buscentre to Portrush and Coleraine via the coast road. There are trains from Belfast Central Station to Coleraine, where you can pick up another train or bus to your destination. **Caledonian MacBrayne** (✆ 028 2076 9299 ⓦ www.calmac.co.uk) run around six ferries a day from Ballycastle to Rathlin Island during the summer months.

SIGHTS & ATTRACTIONS

Antrim Coast Road

The drive along the coastal road is breathtaking, with its craggy cliffs, pretty bays, glens and picturesque villages. You can drive along the coast on the A2 from Larne to Ballycastle, continuing along the coastal road after Cushendall or going cross-country to explore the Glens. Cushendall and Cushendun are among the prettiest villages. ⓐ A2 Antrim Coast Road ⓝ Bus: Antrim Coaster (252), drive or tour

Bushmills Distillery

The oldest licensed whiskey distillery in the world, with a history dating back to 1608. You can take a tour round the distillery but it can get very busy; tickets are sold on a first-come, first-served basis. ⓐ Main Street, Bushmills ⓣ 028 2073 1521 ⓦ www.bushmills.com ⓛ 09.30–16.00 Mon–Sat, 12.00–16.00 Sun Mar–Oct ⓝ Bus: Bushmills. Admission charge

Carrick-a-Rede Rope Bridge

Fight your fear of heights and take the challenge of walking across this rope bridge. Actually it is much better than the original, which only had a single handrail. It was constructed by fishermen who wanted to cross to the rocky island to fish for salmon, but it was eventually taken over by the National Trust, which added the much safer bridge seen here today. Some people make it over to the other side only to panic and not be able to return – until the wardens tell them they will be winched up into a helicopter and then presented with the bill! ⓐ Whitepark Road, Ballintoy

☎ 028 2076 9839 Ⓦ www.nationaltrust.org.uk ⏰ 10.00–18.30 (last tickets at 17.15) Feb–May, Sept & Oct; 10.00–19.30 (last tickets at 18.15) June–Aug (all opening hours are weather permitting). Admission charge

Carrickfergus Castle

A dominant feature of the coastal town of Carrickfergus and the site of many a battle, the castle has a colourful history dating back 800 years. The English retreated here during Edward the Bruce's invasion and during the 14th century it fell to the Scots after a long siege. Over the years it has been used as a prison, a magazine, an armoury and an air-raid shelter. ⓐ Marine Highway ☎ 028 9335 1273 Ⓦ www.ehsni.gov.uk ⏰ 10.00–16.00 Mon–Sat, 14.00–16.00 Sun Oct–Mar; 10.00–18.00 Mon–Sat, 14.00–18.00 Sun Apr–Sept Ⓝ Train: Carrickfergus. Admission charge

⬤ *The hair-raising Carrick-a-Rede Rope Bridge*

Dunluce Castle

The ruins of this medieval castle perch on the edge of the North Antrim cliffs between Bushmills and Portrush. During a storm in 1639, a whole section of the castle collapsed into the sea, killing the cooks and kitchen staff. The castle was abandoned and over time the entire building fell into disrepair. There's a visitor centre and shop, and tours round the castle. ⓐ A2 Coast Road between Bushmills and Portrush ❶ 028 2073 1938 ❶ 028 2073 2850 ⓔ dunluce.castle@doeni.gov.uk ❶ 10.00–17.00 ❶ Drive or tour bus only. Admission charge

Giant's Causeway

A must-see for anyone visiting the province, Giant's Causeway is one of Northern Ireland's top attractions and a UNESCO World Heritage Site. Until geologists came up with scientific theories on the origins of the strange hexagonal basalt columns, the area was steeped in myth and legend. The most famous story surrounds Fionn McCumhaill (McCool), a giant who fell in love with a Scottish belle and created a pathway to reach her. In reality, it's thought to have been the result of volcanic eruptions and the subsequent cooling of the lava by the sea. In total there are around 40,000 columns of varying heights. Look out for the Giant's Boot, Organ, Chimney Stack and Camel's Back, among other features. You can walk the route from the visitor centre down to the Causeway and ascend the cliffs, returning along the top. Alternatively there is a bus that will take you to and from the main site. ⓐ Two miles east of Bushmills ❶ 028 2073 1582 (visitor centre) ❶ 028 2073 2963 (National Trust) ❶ www.nationaltrust.org.uk

◯ *Romantic Dunluce Castle*

🕙 10.00–17.00 Ⓝ Train: Belfast Bridge Street to Giant's Causeway
The Nook Main

Giant's Causeway & Bushmills Railway

Running on the route of the original Causeway Tram, which closed
in 1949, the line re-opened in 2002. Riding the narrow-gauge
steam train is a great way to travel between the two attractions.
There are picnic areas, toilets, café and car park at the Giant's
Causeway Station. A service is usually run during St Patrick's
weekend, Easter, weekends from Easter until June, daily during
July and August and weekends during September and October.
ⓐ Runkerry Road, Bushmills ❶ 028 2073 2844. Admission charge

Nine Glens of Antrim – Glenarm, Glencloy, Glenariff, Glenballyemon, Glenaan, Glencorp, Glendun, Glenshesk and Glentaisie

From the Antrim plateau to the Antrim Coast Road, the nine
green Glens of Antrim are a rich mix of waterfalls, rivers, lush
forests, peat bogs, flora and fauna. Glenariff Forest Park is one
of the most beautiful areas, with trails leading past scenic
mountain viewpoints. ⓐ Antrim Coast Ⓝ Bus: Antrim Coaster;
Car: A2

Portrush

A favourite holiday destination, Portrush is set in a wide
sweeping bay with sandy beaches. Local attractions include
Waterworld indoor water facility, Barry's Amusements (largest
amusement park in Ireland) and the Countryside Centre
(interactive marine exhibits). There's also surfing on the Blue

THE GLENS OF ANTRIM: LAND OF MYTHS

Many legends have circulated the Glens of Antrim, from the Giant Fionn McCool to the Children of Lir (who were turned into swans by their evil stepmother Aiofe). Make a detour from the Glenariff Forest Park to visit Slemish Mountain, where St Patrick is said to have tended Miliucc's sheep after he was captured and brought to Ireland. Watch out for the Watershee, a female fairy who is said to sing sweet songs to lure travellers into lakes and bogs before drowning them. And remember, never cut down a hawthorn tree or you'll upset the fairy folk and bad luck will surely follow. Whether you believe it or not, you'll find magical scenery and plenty of birdwatching, fishing and hiking.

Flag beaches, fishing on or off shore, tennis, bowling, golf at Royal Portrush, and coastal walking and cycling routes. ⓐ North Antrim Coast Ⓝ Bus: Dunluce Avenue

Rathlin Island

Located six miles offshore from Ballycastle, Rathlin Island is eight miles long and less than a mile wide. A birdwatchers' paradise, this is home to Northern Ireland's largest seabird colony – look out for razorbills, fulmars and puffins from the RSPB viewpoint at the West Light. This is just one of three lighthouses on the island, as the wild coastline has led to numerous shipwrecks over the years (about 40). ⓐ Six miles off Ballycastle ☎ 028 7032 7960 or 0774 556 6924 to arrange a tour with Paul Quinn ⛴ Ferry: Ballycastle to Rathlin Island

Whitepark Bay & Ballintoy

This beautiful sweeping bay runs between Portbradden and Ballintoy and is one of the most popular walking routes in the area. The path winds along the basalt cliff top. Ballintoy itself is a picturesque village with its iconic white church and a limestone harbour sheltered by the cliffs behind. ⌖ North Antrim Coast ⛴ Bus: Ballintoy

FESTIVALS

Some of the best festivals during the year include: Coleraine Community and Arts Festival with a programme of cultural activities and music (June); Larne Alive Festival, a month-long event with music, train rides, steam engines and circus acts (June); Feis na Gleann, a traditional Irish music festival throughout the glens (June); Ballycastle Fleadh, a weekend of traditional song and dance (June); Medieval Lughnasa Fayre in Carrickfergus with costumed performers (July); Heart of the Glens Festival in Cushendall with local singing and dance (August); and the Ould Lammas Fair in Ballycastle, one of the oldest in Ireland with livestock sales and stalls selling dulse, dried edible seaweed, and yelloman, a very sugary candy not unlike rock.

TAKING A BREAK

Many of the accommodation options below also have restaurants but there are cafés and bars in every village along the Antrim

Coast Road serving both lunch and dinner. Cushendall and Cushendun are among the prettiest villages, but there's more choice in places like Carrickfergus, Larne, Ballycastle and Portrush. Some of the main attractions, such as Giant's Causeway and Carrick-a-Rede Rope Bridge have cafés where you can stop for refreshments.

AFTER DARK

RESTAURANTS & BARS

55° North £ Split-level family restaurant overlooking the sea which serves a wide range of contemporary dishes, from risotto of pan-seared scallops to braised lamb. **ⓐ** 1 Causeway Street, Portrush **ⓣ** 028 7082 2811 **ⓦ** www.55-north.com **ⓛ** 12.00–15.00, 17.30–21.00 Tues–Fri, 10.00–21.00 Sat, 12.30–19.30 Sun

The Distillers Arms £ Comfy pub in Bushmills where you can stop for a pint in front of the fire with lunch or dinner menus including seafood chowder, fish and chips and home-cured Irish salmon. **ⓐ** Main Street **ⓣ** 028 2073 1044 **ⓦ** www.distillersarms.com **ⓛ** 12.00–late, food served 12.30–15.00 & 17.00–21.00, summer; 17.00–late Mon–Fri, 11.00–late Sat & Sun, food served 17.30–21.00 Wed–Sat, 12.30–15.00 Sat & Sun, winter

The Manor House £ A former Georgian gentleman's house, today it is a guesthouse and restaurant serving fresh fish. Dinner should be pre-ordered. **ⓐ** Rathlin Island **ⓣ** 028 2076 3964 **ⓦ** www.nationaltrust.org **ⓛ** Dinner served at 19.00

The Nook at the Giant's Causeway £–££ Housed in a former 1850s schoolhouse, this restaurant offers a taste of Ulster and is renowned for its scones. ⓐ 48 Causeway Road ⓣ 028 2073 2993 ⓛ Restaurant: 12.00–21.00, bar: 11.30–23.00 Mon–Sat, 11.30–22.00 Sun

Central Bar ££ Downstairs there's a restored traditional bar dating back to 1861 with regular traditional music and live bands. Upstairs has been transformed into a funky restaurant and wine bar serving modern Irish cuisine. ⓐ 12 Ann Street, Ballycastle ⓣ 028 2076 3877 ⓦ www.centralbar.net ⓛ Restaurant: 12.00–21.00, downstairs bar: 11.30–23.30

ACCOMMODATION

HOTELS AND GUESTHOUSES

The Burn £ Comfortable B&B in picturesque Cushendall. ⓐ 63 Ballyemon Road, Cushendall ⓣ 028 2177 1733 ⓦ www.theburn-guesthouse.com ⓔ theburn63@hotmail.com

The Causeway Hotel ££ B&B-style accommodation located right on the doorstep of Giant's Causeway, with superb views. ⓐ 40 Causeway Road, Bushmills ⓣ 028 2073 1210 ⓕ 028 2073 2552 ⓦ www.giants-causeway-hotel.com

Smugglers Inn ££ B&B near Giant's Causeway with a restaurant and bar. ⓐ 306 Whitepark Road ⓣ 028 2073 1577 ⓦ www.smugglers-inn.co.uk ⓔ jenny@smugglers-inn.co.uk

Ballygally Castle £££ Located on the Antrim Coast Road at the foot of the Glens of Antrim, this hotel looks out to the Irish Sea. Part of the hotel dates back to the 17th century and is said to be haunted by a friendly ghost. ⓐ Coast Road, Ballygally ⓣ 028 2858 1066 ⓦ www.hastingshotels.com

The Marine Hotel £££ Comfortable hotel overlooking Ballycastle's new harbour and marina, with restaurant, bar and entertainment. ⓐ 1–3 North Street, Ballycastle ⓣ 028 2076 2222 ⓦ www.marinehotel.net

CAMPING AND HOSTELS
Cushendall Caravan Park £ Camping on the Antrim Coast Road. ⓐ 62 Coast Road, Cushendall ⓣ 028 2177 1699

Cushendun Caravan Park £ Small, family-run caravan park further along the coast. ⓐ 14 Glendun Road, Cushendun ⓣ 028 2176 1254

Mill Rest Youth Hostel £ Cheap and basic accommodation for those on a budget. ⓐ 49 Main Street, Bushmills ⓣ 028 2073 1222 ⓦ www.hini.org.uk

---

ⓘ *Belfast Welcome Centre: find out all you need to know*

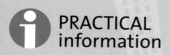

PRACTICAL
information

Directory

GETTING THERE

By air

Aer Lingus operates daily flights between Belfast International and London Heathrow. BMI Baby operates several flights a day between Belfast International Airport and Birmingham, Cardiff, Manchester and Nottingham East Midlands, and between George Best Belfast City Airport and London Heathrow. easyJet operates several flights a day between Belfast International and Bristol, Edinburgh, Glasgow, Liverpool, London (Gatwick, Luton and Stansted) and Newcastle. Jet2.com operates daily flights between Belfast International, Blackpool and Leeds Bradford. Manx2.com operates daily (except Sat) flights from Belfast City Airport to Blackpool and Gloucester, and several daily flights to the Isle of Man. It also operates one a week between Belfast International and Blackpool, and daily (except Sat) flights to the Isle of Man. British Airways operates several flights a day between George Best Belfast City Airport and Manchester. Flybe operates several flights a day between Belfast City and Aberdeen, Birmingham, Cardiff, Doncaster Sheffield, Dundee, Edinburgh, Exeter, Glasgow, Inverness, Jersey, Leeds Bradford, London Gatwick, Manchester, Newcastle, Newquay and Southampton, and one a day to and from Bristol. Ryanair operates daily flights between Belfast City and London Stansted, Glasgow Prestwick, Liverpool and East Midlands.

Aer Lingus ✆ 0870 876 5000 ⓦ www.aerlingus.com

BMI Baby ✆ 08702 642229 ⓦ www.bmibaby.com

British Airways ✆ 0870 850 9850 ⓦ www.ba.com

easyJet ⓣ 0871 244 2366 ⓦ www.easyjet.com

flybe ⓣ 0871 700 0535 ⓦ www.flybe.com

et2.com ⓣ 0871 226 1737 ⓦ www.jet2.com

Manx2.com ⓣ 0870 242 2226 ⓦ www.manx2.com

Ryanair ⓣ 0871 246 0000 ⓦ www.ryanair.com

Many people are aware that air travel emits CO_2, which contributes to climate change. You may be interested in the possibility of lessening the environmental impact of your flight through the charity **Climate Care** (ⓦ www.climatecare.org), which offsets your CO_2 by funding environmental projects around the world.

By rail

Services to Belfast run from Bangor, Derry City and Portrush, Larne and Portadown. There's also the cross-border Enterprise service with Iarnród Éireann eight times a day between Belfast and Dublin with main Northern Ireland stops at Derry, Coleraine, Belfast Central, Lisburn, Portadown and Newry.

By road

Scottish Citylink runs services between Belfast's Europa Buscentre and various Scottish cities (ⓦ www.citylink.co.uk). **National Express** runs services between the Europa Buscentre and several English and Welsh cities (ⓦ www.nationalexpress.com).

Belfast is 113 km (70 miles) from Derry by A roads and the M2 motorway, 100 miles from Dublin and 422 km (262 miles) from Cork on toll-paying motorways, A roads and the M1 motorway into Belfast city centre.

By water

There are several ferry routes from the rest of the UK that come into Belfast ferry port close to the city centre and Larne (37 km, or 23 miles, north of Belfast). **Stena Line** operates regular Belfast–Stranraer, Belfast–Troon and Larne (north of Belfast)–Fleetwood services (Ⓦ www.stenaline.co.uk). **Steam Packet** operates a Belfast–Douglas (Isle of Man) service (Ⓦ www.steam-packet.com). **P&O Irish Sea Ferries** operates Larne–Troon and Larne–Cairnryan services (Ⓦ www.poirishsea.com). **Norfolkline Irish Sea** operates a Belfast–Liverpool service (Ⓦ www.norfolkline-ferries.co.uk).

ENTRY FORMALITIES

Citizens of the rest of the UK need some form of photographic ID (usually a valid passport or driving licence). Citizens of EU countries, USA, Canada, Australia, New Zealand and South Africa do not require a visa if coming to Northern Ireland (or the rest of the UK) as a visitor.

Visitors to the UK and Northern Ireland are entitled to bring the following duty paid goods into the country for their own personal use: up to 3,200 cigarettes, 400 cigarillos, 200 cigars, 3 kg of smoking tobacco, 10 litres of spirits, 90 litres of wine (60 litres of sparkling wine), 20 litres of fortified wine and 110 litres of beer. However, if you are questioned by Customs officials and cannot satisfy them that it is not for commercial use, it could be seized and not returned. Exceptions apply to the following EU countries: from Estonia, 200 cigarettes or 250 g of smoking tobacco (no restrictions on other tobacco products if for your own use); from Bulgaria, Hungary, Latvia, Lithuania, Poland, Slovakia and Slovenia, 200 cigarettes (no restrictions on other tobacco products if for your own use).

If you are travelling from non-EU countries you have a duty free allowance of 200 cigarettes or 100 cigarillos or 50 cigars or 250 g of tobacco; 2 litres of still table wine; 1 litre of spirits or strong liqueurs over 22% volume or 2 litres of fortified wine, sparkling wine or other liqueurs; 60 cc/ml of perfume; 250 cc/ml of eau de toilette and £145 worth of all other goods including gifts and souvenirs.

MONEY

As with the rest of the UK, in Northern Ireland the currency is UK pounds sterling. Northern Ireland has four clearing banks – Bank of Ireland, First Trust, Northern Bank and Ulster Bank, which print their own bank notes. These are valid sterling notes in the same denominations as the rest of the UK (£5, £10, £20 and £50) but it's advisable to change them to English notes if you're moving on to England as many places don't like to accept them, despite their legality. Most banks have ATMs and are located throughout the city centre, main commercial areas of the city and all towns throughout the province. Larger banks in Belfast have Bureaux de Change, but you can also try travel agencies, the Belfast Welcome Centre, some Tourist Information Centres, large hotels and some tourist attractions.

Credit cards are generally accepted in most shops, restaurants, bars and attractions, but if there's any doubt, it is best to check first to avoid any embarrassment.

HEALTH, SAFETY & CRIME

There should be absolutely no problem with the drinking water in Belfast – the main supply comes from the Mourne Mountains to the city. Likewise, there should be no problem with the city's food.

The public health-care system in Northern Ireland is part of the UK National Health Service (NHS) but here it integrates both health and social care into one system, so citizens of the UK are covered for health care. As part of a reciprocal agreement, citizens of the EU are entitled to reduced-cost and sometimes free medical treatment if they have a European Health Insurance Card (EHIC). You can apply for this in your country of citizenship. Make sure you have ID with you as well as your EHIC.

As this may not cover all your medical needs, it is always better have your own private travel insurance to pay for repatriation, should you need it. Insurance also usually covers you if you are a victim of crime, but check your policy carefully before you travel.

Northern Ireland has one of the lowest crime rate in Europe. Even during The Troubles tourists were rarely targeted or directly affected. Just use your common sense as you would when travelling anywhere – don't take too much cash out with you, don't flash expensive jewellery around or walk along the street with a big open map. It can also get quite rowdy at the weekends along the Golden Mile and Botanic but most people are just happy after a few drinks. However, if you're lost or feel uncomfortable it's better to ask someone for directions during the day – most people are happy to help – or take a taxi home if it's late, **Fon A Cab** (☎ 028 9023 3333). If you do have an emergency, call the police, ambulance or fire service on 999. For lost valuables call the **PSNI (Police Service of Northern Ireland) Police Lost Property** (☎ 0845 600 8000 non-emergency police number). Alternatively you can call into Musgrave Police Station on Ann Street (by Queen's Bridge) for this or other matters.

OPENING HOURS

Shops usually open from Monday to Saturday 09.30–17.30 with late-night shopping on Thursday (21.00). Larger stores and most high-street stores in Belfast city centre also open on Sunday from 13.00–18.00. Banks generally open from Monday to Friday 09.30–16.30 but some also open on Saturday mornings. They are always closed on Sundays and public holidays.

TOILETS

There are several public toilets in the city centre either as standalones in the street or in car parks, bus stations (Europa and Laganside Buscentres), shopping centres and markets, including CastleCourt on Royal Avenue. You can also find clean

▲ *The city centre is easy to navigate*

toilets in department stores and museums, and McDonald's in
Royal Avenue is also widely used, although it's not the cleanest
of places. In an emergency you can also go into pubs and cafés,
but you usually have to buy something.

CHILDREN

Children are welcomed and allowed in more establishments
than in England, but in general they are not allowed in bars
and pubs, unless they serve food as well (the bars, not the kids).

Children should love going on sightseeing bus tours, boat
trips and to the Odyssey Centre (see pages 94–5), where there's
all-day entertainment, including the W5 interactive discovery
centre and the Pavilion. A great fresh-air idea is Belfast Castle
and Cave Hill Country Park (see page 82). If there aren't any
events on at the castle you can have a look around, then take
the kids on a nature trail through Cave Hill Country Park up to
the gloriously named Napoleon's Nose. Titanic Boat Tours allow
kids to discover something about the Titanic and enjoy the short
boat trip at the same time (see page 96).

COMMUNICATIONS
Internet
Belfast is well wired. The Belfast Welcome Centre (see page 136)
is a reliable and pleasant place to check those stress-inducing
emails from the boss.

Phone
Coin- and card-operated telephone booths can be found all over
the city. Phone cards can be purchased at tobacconists and

TELEPHONING THE UK

The Belfast and other Northern Ireland numbers in this book include the Northern Ireland number (028) followed by an area code and a six-digit number. Within Northern Ireland you don't need to dial 028 but you do need to dial the rest of the digits.

TELEPHONING ABROAD

To phone anywhere else you should dial the national code first (353 Republic of Ireland, 1 USA or Canada, 61 Australia, 64 New Zealand, 72 South Africa) plus the area code (minus the 0 if there is one) and the rest of the number. For international operator assistance call 155.

supermarkets. All phones can be used to call abroad – it's cheaper before 08.00, after 18.00 and at weekends.

Post

Post offices are generally open from 09.00–17.30 Monday–Friday and 09.00–12.00 on Saturday. The main post office in Belfast city centre is at Castle Junction. You can post your letters at post offices or in the red post boxes around the city and the rest of Northern Ireland. Stamps can be bought at post offices, tobacconists, supermarkets and some tourist offices and petrol stations.

ELECTRICITY

As with the rest of the UK and Republic of Ireland, the current is

240V (50Hz) and three-pin plugs are used. Visitors from outside the UK or Ireland will need an adaptor.

TRAVELLERS WITH DISABILITIES

To stay in line with EU regulations, facilities are being improved in Northern Ireland as with the rest of the UK. Work on some venues has already taken place (Grand Opera House and large hotels and restaurants), providing wheelchair access via ramps or lifts. Sources of advice for travellers with disabilities include:

Shopmobility Belfast ⓐ Westgate House, 2 Queen Street ⓣ 028 9080 8090 ⓦ www.shopmobilitybelfast.co.uk
Disability Action ⓐ 189 Airport Road West ⓣ 028 9029 7880 ⓦ www.disabilityaction.org

TOURIST INFORMATION

Belfast has a very helpful tourist office in the city centre as well as two at Belfast International and George Best Belfast City Airport.

Belfast Welcome Centre ⓐ 47 Donegall Place ⓣ 028 9024 6609 ⓕ 028 9031 2424 ⓔ info@belfastvisitor.com ⓛ 09.00–17.30 Mon–Sat Oct–May; 09.00–19.00 Mon–Sat, 12.00–17.00 Sun June–Sept
Useful websites include the official tourism website for Belfast, ⓦ www.gotobelfast.com and
ⓦ www.discovernorthernireland.com

BACKGROUND READING

Great Hatred, Little Room: Making Peace in Northern Ireland by Jonathan Powell. An insider's account of the triumph of sacrifice, diplomacy and compromise that achieved what many had given up as impossible: the provision of peace to this beautiful city.

Made in Belfast by Vivienne Pollock and Trevor Parkhill. A good overview of life, work and industry, from the linen mills and shipbuilding to entertainments, with plenty of old photographs.

Troubled Images: Posters and Images of the Northern Ireland Conflict from the Linen Hall Library, Belfast by Yvonne Murphy, Allan Leonard, Gordon Gillespie and Kris Brown. This excellent collection contains some truly breathtaking illustrations of the city's long history of internecine struggle.

War as a Way of Life by John Conroy. An intimate account of growing up in West Belfast.

Watching the Door by Kevin Myers. A brilliantly executed, laugh-out-loud account of a young man's romp through the city during The Troubles.

The Wee Wild One: Stories of Belfast and Beyond by Ruth C Schwertfiger. A fresh view on the city through literature and strange tales.

Emergencies

EMERGENCY NUMBERS

For emergencies requiring police, fire or ambulance services call ☎ 999

MEDICAL SERVICES

Only call 999 in an absolute emergency. If you can, ask a pharmacist for help or visit a doctor's surgery. In case of emergency you should ask to be taken to the nearest hospital. The Royal has a specialist hospital just for children, as well as maternity and dentistry hospitals. Citizens of the UK are entitled to full medical treatment and holders of EHIC cards (see page 132) are entitled to basic medical treatment. Still, travel insurance with a good level of medical cover is advisable for repatriation and essential for non-EU visitors.

Emergency medical services are very good in Northern Ireland and often the waiting time in Accident and Emergency is less than in other parts of the UK. You should try and provide as much information as possible about the patient, including personal details and the symptoms. If you are physically able, go to A&E (Accident and Emergency) at the nearest hospital or ask the hotel or pharmacist for the number of a local doctor, clinic or dentist.

Belfast City Hospital ⓐ 51 Lisburn Road ☎ 028 9032 9241
Mater Hospital Trust ⓐ 45–51 Crumlin Road ☎ 028 9074 1211
Royal Victoria Hospital ⓐ 274 Grosvenor Road ☎ 028 9024 0503
Shaftesbury Square Hospital ⓐ 116–120 Great Victoria Street ☎ 028 9032 9808

POLICE

If you are unlucky enough to be the victim of crime, you should call the **PSNI** (Police Service of Northern Ireland, ☎ 0845 600 8000). Only call 999 in absolute emergencies, otherwise contact the police station directly on foot or by phone. If you lose some property or have something stolen then you should report this to the lost property office at Musgrave Police Station. You'll be given an official report to help make any necessary insurance claims. It is advisable to take some photographic ID with you when you make the report.

Musgrave Police Station @ Ann Street

EMBASSIES & CONSULATES

Australian High Commission @ Australia House, Strand, London WC28 4LA ☎ 020 7379 4334

Canadian Consulate @ Unit 3, Ormeau Business Park ☎/📠 028 9127 2060

New Zealand Honorary Consul @ 118A Lisburn Road, Crumlin ☎ 028 9264 8098

South African High Commission @ South Africa House, Trafalgar Square, London ☎ 020 7925 8900 📠 020 7925 8930

US Consulate @ Danesfort House, 223 Stranmillis Road ☎ 028 9038 6100 📠 028 9068 1301